An Anatomy of Drama

MARTIN ESSLIN

AN ANATOMY OF DRAMA

TEMPLE SMITH·LONDON

Also by Martin Esslin

Brecht: A Choice of Evils
The Theatre of the Absurd
Brief Chronicles
Pinter: A Study of his Plays
Artaud

Edited by Martin Esslin

The Genius of the German Theatre
Samuel Beckett: A Collection of Critical Essays
The New Theatre of Europe 4

First published in Great Britain 1976
by Maurice Temple Smith Ltd
37 Great Russell Street, London WC1
© 1976 Martin Esslin
ISBN 0 85117 1087

Typesetting by Print Origination
Merseyside
Printed in Great Britain by
Billing & Son Ltd
London, Guildford and Worcester

Contents

Foreword

A great deal is written about the theatre and drama: and much of it is rich in subtle insights, brilliant theories and illuminating discoveries about the structure and meaning of plays. Yet one basic question usually still remains open: why should those concerned with the art resort to drama rather than any other form of communication, what is the underlying, basic nature of the dramatic form and what is it that drama can express better than any other medium of human communication?

This is the question I have tried to answer in this book. In writing it I have tried to keep my mind free from the many theories and systems of aesthetics with which I am only too familiar through my work as a critic and scholar concerned with drama. I have, instead, endeavoured to draw as far as that was humanly possible on my practical experience as a director of drama. It is one thing for a scholar to say that a play is fascinatingly interesting, quite another to take the decision actually to put it into production and to offer it to a general public. As head of a production unit responsible for something like a thousand such decisions each year (the radio drama department of the BBC) it is only natural that the second, the practical and pragmatic, consideration prevails for me. And as a working director I am equally compelled to think of the plays I am confronted with in terms of practice rather than theory: how to make them *work*. Most practical and pragmatic decisions of this kind are based on experience which has become second nature and which operates on an almost subconscious level. What I have here tried to do is to raise the essential content of that instinctive, experiential knowledge to the level of consciousness, capable—I hope—of being communicated.

I make no claim that the insights this effort has produced differ, essentially, from much that is accepted academic doctrine. But perhaps the process of reasoning and recall of past experience through which they have been reached may make the old, established insights appear in a new light; and a few new angles may even be added to their understanding. Where my conclusions differ from established academic thinking, they might perhaps lead to a new look being taken at some aspects of it; after all, theories must from time to time be tested through practical experience.

At the same time, because I have tried to keep to simple and basic considerations, I hope the book may serve as a useful introduction to the study as well as practice of drama.

The first impulse to write such an introduction came when I was asked by the Open University to contribute some talks to their drama course. I am grateful to Dr Helen Rapp of the BBC's Open University unit who acted as producer for these radio talks and greatly helped me with advice and criticism.

London, April 1976   Martin Esslin

1 Definitions, delimitations

Many thousands of volumes have been written about drama and yet there does not seem to exist one generally acceptable definition of the term. 'A composition in prose or verse', says my edition of the Oxford Dictionary, 'adapted to be acted on the stage, in which a story is related by means of dialogue and action, and is represented, with accompanying gesture, costume and scenery, as in real life; a play.' Not only is this long–winded and clumsily put; it is also downright incorrect. 'A *composition* in prose or verse' seems to imply a text previously composed, so this definition cannot apply to an improvised dramatic performance; '...in which a story is related *by means of dialogue*...': what, then, about those exquisite mime dramas with which the crowds of Paris were being entertained in the nineteenth century or which artists like Marcel Marceau give us today? '...adapted to be *acted on the stage*...': and what about drama in television, radio or the cinema? '...represented with accompanying gesture, *costume and scenery*...': gestures, yes; but I have seen very good drama without costume or indeed scenery! '...as in *real life*...': now, that is going a little far. It seems to assume that all drama must be realistic drama. Is *Waiting for Godot,* or for that matter *The Merry Widow,* like real life? And yet both, undoubtedly, are drama.

Other dictionary definitions I have looked up have proved equally misleading and incorrect. For the fact is that the art, activity, human craving or instinct which embodies itself in drama is so deeply enmeshed in human nature itself, and in a multitude of human pursuits, that it is wellnigh impossible to draw the exact dividing line between where one kind of more general activity stops and drama proper starts.

One can, for example, look at drama as a manifestation of the *play instinct*: children playing Mother and Father or Cowboys and Indians are, in some sense, improvising drama. Or one can see drama as a manifestation of one of humanity's prime social needs, that of *ritual*: tribal dances, religious services, great state occasions all contain strong dramatic elements. Or one can look at drama as something one goes to *see,* which is being presented and organised as something to be seen, a *spectacle*: in Greek *theatre (...theatron)* means a place where one goes to *see* something: the triumphal entry of a victorious emperor into Rome contained dramatic elements, so did gladiatorial contests between Christians and lions, so did public executions, so do all spectator sports. None of these activities can be regarded as drama in its proper sense, but the dividing lines between them and drama are very fluid indeed: is a circus, for example, where acrobats display their prowess a sporting activity? What then of the clowns who perform acrobatic feats together with little farcical scenes? What of the riders who display their skill in a simulated attack on a stage-coach? Johann Wolfgang von Goethe, the prince of German poets, resigned his post as artistic director of the Court Theatre at Weimar in protest against a play involving the feats of a performing

10

dog. He may have been quite right in doing so, but was not his definition of drama a little narrow, nevertheless? Is drama no longer drama when not all the actors are human beings? What, then, of puppet theatre and shadow plays (like those of Java), what of cartoon films in which the actors are mere drawings?

Perhaps one should approach the definition of drama from that angle: there is no drama without *actors*, whether they are present in flesh and blood, or projected shadows upon a screen, or puppets. 'Enacted fiction' might be a short and pithy definition of drama, except that it would exclude documentary drama, which is enacted reality. Perhaps 'an art form based on mimetic action' would fit the bill? But then there are abstract ballets or, indeed, cartoon films, which while still action are not, strictly speaking, mimetic. Are they still drama? Yes, in one sense; no, in another.

Definitions—and thinking about definitions—are valuable and essential, but they must never be made into absolutes; if they are, they become obstacles to the organic development of new forms, experiment and invention. It is precisely because an activity like drama has fluid delimitations that it can continuously renew itself from sources that had hitherto been regarded as lying beyond its limits. It does not really matter whether the circus or the music hall, the political procession or the pop concert might still be strictly defined as forms of drama. What is certain is that the art of drama has received important, sometimes overwhelmingly significant inspirations and impulses from them. And similarly out of more strictly defined forms of drama may come new developments like the Happening or the multimedia show; there will be much debate about whether these should then still be called drama; such debate will be

11

valuable in the process of clarification of ideas and methods, but its actual outcome—is it drama, is it not?—will be relatively unimportant.

There is, however, one basic point of fundamental importance which has to be stressed because, although obvious, it continues to be persistently overlooked, particularly by those who as critics and academic teachers of drama are the guardians of its tradition and lore: and that is that theatre—stage drama—is, in the second half of the twentieth century, only one—and a relatively minor—form of dramatic expression and that the mechanically reproduced drama of the mass media, the cinema, television and radio, different though it may be in some of its techniques, is also fundamentally drama and obeys the same basic principles of the psychology of perception and understanding from which all the techniques of dramatic communication derive.

Drama as a technique of communication between human beings has entered upon a completely new phase of development of truly secular importance in an age which the great German critic Walter Benjamin characterised as that of 'the technical reproduceability of works of art'. Those who still regard live theatre as the only true form of drama are comparable to those contemporaries of Gutenberg who would acknowledge only a handwritten book as a true book. Through the mass media drama has become one of the most powerful means of communication between human beings, far more powerful than the merely printed word which was the basis of the Gutenberg revolution.

That is why a knowledge of the nature of drama, an understanding of its fundamental principles and techniques and an ability to think and talk about it critically has become very necessary indeed in our world. And that

Definitions, delimitations

does not only apply to such great works of the human spirit as the plays of Sophocles or Shakespeare, but also to the television situation comedy or, indeed, to that briefest of dramatic forms, the television or radio commercial. We are surrounded by dramatic communication in all the industrialised countries of the world today; we ought to be able to understand and analyse its impact on ourselves—and our children. The explosion of dramatic forms of expression presents us all with considerable risks of being enslaved to insidious forms of subliminal manipulation of our consciousness; but also with immense creative opportunities.

2 The nature of drama

In Greek the word *drama* simply means *action*. Drama is mimetic action, action in imitation or representation of human behaviour (with the exception of the few extreme cases of abstract action which I have mentioned). What is crucial is the emphasis on action. So drama is not simply a form of literature (although the words used in a play, when they are written down, can be treated as literature). What makes drama drama is precisely the element which lies outside and beyond the words and which has to be seen as action—or *acted*—to give the author's concept its full value.

In talking about an art form—and in trying to get the fullest enjoyment and enrichment from it—it is of fundamental importance to understand what this particular art form is specifically able to contribute to the sum total of man's tools of expression and, indeed, to conceptualisation, thought. If in music we are dealing with the ability of sounds to make us recreate the ebb and flow of human emotion; if in architecture and sculpture we are able to explore the expressive possibilities of the arrangement of materials and of masses in space; if literature is concerned with the ways in which we can handle—and respond to—language and concepts; if painting is ulti-

14

mately concerned with the relationship and impact of colours, shapes and textures on a flat surface, what, then, is the specific province of drama? Why, for instance, should we act out an incident rather than merely tell a story about it?

Let me start on a purely personal note. In the '40s and '50s I worked as a script writer in the European Service of the BBC. The programmes we were supposed to write were intended to give an audience who did not speak English an idea of what life in Britain was like. They were supposed to be *documentary* programmes, as near to reality as possible. But if, for example, we wanted to describe how an employment exchange worked, because of the language barrier between our listeners and life in England we could not just go out with a tape recorder and produce a recording of the various things that went on there. I remember being sent to write such a programme. I visited one of the employment exchanges and I was impressed by the mixture of bureaucratic formality with courtesy and real kindness on the part of the civil servants there.

How could I convey my impressions in the best possible manner? I could have written a purely literary, discursive description, something on these lines:

The official asks the applicant for a job to give him the relevant details. He is not unfriendly although he maintains a certain reserve and distance, yet at the same time it is quite apparent from the tone of voice he uses that he is genuinely trying to help the person in front of him...

And so on and so on. Such a description would not have carried much conviction because it would have sounded

15

like very special pleading with a purely propagandist intention. It would also have been extremely longwinded—an endless psychological analysis. So instead I decided to dramatise the little scene:

OFFICIAL: Do sit down.
APPLICANT: Thank you.
OFFICIAL: Now let's see. Your name is —?
APPLICANT: John Smith.
OFFICIAL: And your last job was —
APPLICANT: Machinist.
OFFICIAL: I see.

And so on. When this short dialogue is acted in the right spirit, the tone of voice—the acting, the action—conveys infinitely more than the actual words that are spoken. Indeed, the words (the literary component of the dramatic fragment) are secondary. The real information conveyed in the little scene when acted lies in the *relationship*, the *interaction* of two characters, the way they react to each other. This came across even in radio merely through the tone of voice. On the stage, the way their eyes meet or fail to meet, the way the official might gesture towards a chair when he invites the applicant to sit down, would be equally significant and important. On the page of the script this little dialogue conveys only a very small fraction of what the acted scene will express. This illustrates the importance of actors and directors in the art of drama. It also points to the fact that a really good playwright needs immense skill to convey the mood of the gestures, the tone of voice he wants from his actors through the dialogue he writes. But this leads us into very much more technical and complex areas. Let us, for the moment, stay with the basic concepts.

16

The nature of drama

In the arts, as in philosophy, the principle of Occam's Razor remains of permanent validity—the most economical, the least time-consuming, the most elegant expression of thought will be nearest to the truth. For the expression of the imponderable mood, the hidden tensions and sympathies, the subtleties of human relationships and interaction, drama is by far the most economical means of expression.

Think of it in these terms: a novelist has to describe what a character looks like. In a play the appearance of the character is instantly conveyed by the actor's body and costume and make-up. The other visual elements in drama, the setting, the environment in which the action takes place, can be equally instantly communicated by the sets, the lighting, the grouping of the characters on the stage. (This also applies to the cinema and plays on television.)

These are the most primitive considerations. Far more profound, far more subtle, is the way in which drama can operate on several levels at once. Discursive literature, the novel, the short story, the epic poem, operates at any given instant only along a single dimension. Their storytelling is linear. Complexities, such as ironies or doubletakes, are of course within the range of discursive writing, but they have to be built up through accumulation of the total picture by adding elements from moment to moment. And there is already a high degree of abstraction in any story told in such a manner: the author is constantly seen at work in selecting his material, in deciding which element to introduce next. Drama, by being a concrete representation of action as it actually takes place, is able to show us several aspects of that action simultaneously and also to convey several levels of action and emotion at the same time. For example, a line of dialogue like 'Good morning, my dear friend!' might be spoken in a wide variety of tones of voice and expression. Accordingly, an audience might wonder whether the person who spoke these words meant them sincerely, used them sarcastically, or even had a note of hidden hostility in them. In a novel the author would have to say something along these lines:

> '"Good morning my dear friend," he said, but Jack had the impression that he did not really mean it. Was he sarcastic, he asked himself, or was he suppressing some deeply felt hostility....'

The dramatic form of expression leaves the spectator free to make up his own mind about the sub-text concealed behind the overt text—in other words, it puts him into the same situation as the character to whom the words are addressed. Therefore it makes it possible for him to experience the emotion of the character directly rather then having to accept a mere description of it. Moreover, this need to decide for themselves how to interpret the action also adds to the suspense with which the audience will follow the story. Instead of being told about a situation, as the reader of a novel or story inevitably is, the spectators of drama are actually put into, directly confronted with, the situation concerned.

So we can say that drama is the most concrete form in which art can recreate human situations, human relationships. And this concreteness is derived from the fact that, whereas any narrative form of communication will tend to relate events that have happened in the past and are now finished, the concreteness of drama is happening in an eternal present tense, not there and then, but here and now.

18

The nature of drama

There is a seeming exception to this—the modern narrative technique of the internal monologue in which the novelist puts us inside the mind of his character and follows his thoughts as they occur. But the very term monologue, which comes from drama, shows that the internal monologue is, in fact, a dramatic form as much as a narrative one. Internal monologues are essentially drama; hence they can be acted—and often are, particularly on radio. A writer like Beckett, most of whose narrative works are internal monologues, must really be regarded as, above all, an outstanding dramatic writer, a fact which is borne out by his great success as a writer both for the stage and for radio.

The immediacy and concreteness of drama and the fact that it forces the spectator to interpret what is happening in front of him on a multitude of levels, compelling *him* to decide whether the tone of voice of the character was friendly or menacing or sarcastic, means that drama has all the qualities of the real world, the real situations we meet in life—but with one very decisive difference: in life the situations we are confronted with are real; in the theatre—or in the other forms of drama (radio, TV, the cinema)—they are merely acted, they are make-believe, *play*.

Now the difference between reality and play is that what happens in reality is irreversible, while in play it is possible to start again from scratch. Play is a simulation of reality. That, far from making play a frivolous pastime, in fact emphasises the immense importance of all play activity for the well-being and development of man.

Children play in order to familiarise themselves with the behaviour patterns which they will have to use and experience in their life, in reality. Young animals play to learn to hunt, to flee, to orientate themselves. All play

19

activity of this kind is essentially dramatic, because it consists of a mimesis, an imitation of real-life situations and behaviour patterns. The play instinct is one of the basic human drives, essential for the survival of the individual as well as of the species. So drama can be regarded as more than a mere pastime. It is profoundly linked to the basic make-up of our species.

Yes, you may object, that may be true of the play of children and animals. But is it also true of a comedy by Noel Coward or a Broadway farce?

I would argue that, strange as it may sound, that is indeed the case, however indirectly, at however many removes.

Look at it this way: in their play children try out and learn the roles (note the terminology, which comes from the theatre) they will play in their adult life. Much of the current debate about the equality of women, for example, is concerned with showing that little girls are often brainwashed into an inferior position by learning a certain type of female role in their childhood, largely through being made to play differently from boys. If this is so, it is equally evident that society continues to instruct (or, if you prefer the term, to brainwash) its members in the different social roles they have to play throughout their lives. Drama is one of the most potent instruments of this process of instruction or brainwashing—sociologists would call it the process by which individuals internalize their social roles.

Dramatic forms of presentation—and in our society every individual is exposed to them daily through the mass media—are one of the prime instruments by which society communicates its codes of behaviour to its members. This communication works both by encouraging imitation and by presenting examples of behaviour

20

which has to be avoided or shunned. Here wires may sometimes become crossed: the gangster movie designed to show that crime does not pay may in fact demonstrate to a potential gangster how to go about being a gangster. One way or another it is through the vicarious play activity (which drama is for adults) that many of these patterns are transmitted, in a positive or a negative sense.

The drawing-room comedy à *la* Noel Coward also clearly transmits patterns of behaviour in the form of the manners, the social forms, the sexual codes that are being shown; and equally the bedroom farce, by making people laugh about the outrageous lapses of parsons caught in brothels, also reinforces codes of behaviour. Laughter is a form of release for subconscious anxieties. Farce, as I hope to show later, is about the anxieties which people have about possible lapses of behaviour to which they may be exposed through temptations of various kinds.

But, beyond that, drama can be more than merely an instrument by which society transmits its behaviour patterns to its members. It can also be an instrument of thought, a cognitive process.

For drama is not only the most concrete—that is, the least abstract—artistic imitation of real human behaviour, it is also the most concrete form in which we can think about human situations. The higher the level of abstraction, the more remote thought becomes from human reality. It is one thing to argue that, for example, capital punishment is effective or ineffective, quite another to translate that abstract concept, which may be buttressed by statistics, into human reality. That we can only do by imagining the case of one human being involved in capital punishment—and the best way to do so is to write and act out a play about it. It is no coincidence that the think-tanks trying to work out plans of action for various future contingencies such as epidemics or nuclear wars do this in terms of working out scenarios for the possible sequence of events. In other words they are translating their statistics, their computer data, into dramatic form, into concrete situations which have to be acted out with all the imponderables such as the individual psychological reaction of the decision-makers involved.

Most serious drama from the Greek tragedies to Samuel Beckett is of this nature. It is a form of philosophising, not in abstract but in concrete terms—in today's philosophical jargon one would say in existential terms. It is significant that an important existential philosopher, Jean-Paul Sartre, felt compelled to write plays as well as novels. The dramatic form was the only method by which he could work out some of the concrete implications of his abstract philosophical thought.

Bertolt Brecht, a Marxist, also regarded drama as a scientific method, the theatre as an experimental laboratory for the testing of human behaviour in given situations. 'What would happen if...?' is the premise of most plays of this nature. Most of the social problems of the last hundred years were not only aired but worked out in the plays of writers like Ibsen, Bernard Shaw or Brecht; many profound philosophical problems in the plays of Strindberg, Pirandello, Camus, Sartre and Beckett.

But—you may object—in a play these problems are worked out arbitrarily according to the whim of a playwright. In a laboratory they are tested objectively.

I am convinced that this possibility also exists in the theatre. For, in the theatre too, there are objective ways of testing experiments in human behaviour.

3 Drama as collective experience: ritual

Drama, therefore, can be seen as a form of thought, a cognitive process, a method by which we can translate abstract concepts into concrete human terms or by which we can set up a situation and work out its consequences (for example: what would happen if, say, all extramarital love were to become a capital offence, as in Shakespeare's *Measure for Measure*).

Yet are not the playwright, the director, the actors so completely in control of a dramatic experiment of this kind that they can arbitrarily dictate its result, make it come out just as they like? And how, if that is so, can drama be regarded as a way of testing the consequences and implications of a given situation?

The author and the performers are only one half of the total process: the other half is the audience and its reaction. Without an audience there is no drama. A play which is not performed is merely literature. In performance a play either works or it doesn't work, which is to say that the audience either finds it acceptable or not. As I tried to show in the previous chapter, drama compels the spectator to decode what he sees on the stage in exactly the same way as he has to make sense of, or interpret, any event he encounters in his personal life. He sees and hears what the ghost tells Hamlet and he, just as Hamlet himself, has to make up his mind whether that ghost is genuine or merely an evil spirit sent to tempt Hamlet into sin. So the spectator is made to experience what the character on the stage undergoes. And he will very soon be able to judge whether that experience feels right. In other words, anything that the author and the actors present to their audience will either carry conviction or not.

That is not to say that the audience must, as it were, agree with Nora in Ibsen's *A Doll's House* that to leave her husband is the right thing; but they will undoubtedly sense whether the marital situation set up by Ibsen is, as a situation, basically real or not. Even those who violently object to Nora's action will have been compelled to reformulate their attitude to marriage, to rethink it in the terms of the problem faced by Nora and her husband. Moveover—and this is one of the most attractive and mysterious characteristics of drama—some sort of collective reaction, a consensus, will often develop in an audience, and will in a stage performance tend to become manifest both to the actors and to the audience itself. Anyone who has ever acted on a stage will confirm that the collective reaction to a play is palpably real. The audience, in some senses, ceases to be an assemblage of isolated individuals; it becomes a collective consciousness. There is nothing mystical about this. After all, if they are concentrating on the same action in front of their eyes, all these people, identifying with the action and the characters on the stage, are inevitably also responding to each other: it can be said that they all have the same thought in their minds (the thought which is being expressed on the stage) and experience something like the same emotion. They are all equally terrified as Dracula unexpectedly rises from his coffin, all equally disgusted when Jean kills the canary in Strindberg's *Miss Julie,* all equally amused as the comedian cracks his joke. If they all gasp in terror or disgust at the same moment, all laugh loudly at the same moment, the actors experience this as a very powerful reaction from what must seem to them a many-headed monster with but one mind. They can clearly feel the tension if the audience is tense, just as they can clearly feel its boredom when the audience, having lost concentration, begins to cough or fidget.

Positive reaction from the audience has a powerful effect on the actors, and so has negative reaction. If the audience fails to laugh at jokes, the actors will instinctively play them more broadly, underline them, signal more clearly that what they are saying is funny. If the audience responds, the actors will be inspired by the response and this in turn will elicit more and more powerful responses from the audience. This is the famous feed-back effect between the stage and the audience. But there is another equally powerful feed-back: between the individual members of the audience themselves. Laughter, for instance, is known to be infectious. A few people in the audience, who are quicker than the others in seeing a joke, can set off gales of laughter in all the rest. Seeing your neighbour in the seat next to you roar with merriment will set you off, and your merriment will in turn reinforce his. People who are alone reading a book, or watching television, on the whole do not laugh uproariously. Nor do they cheer wildly at patriotic sentiments they might find in the book or see on the screen. That is why comedy shows in radio or TV are produced with a studio audience or even canned laughter—so that the lone television viewer or radio listener can experience

25

something of the infectiousness of collective laughter; that is why Hitler never spoke just into a microphone but insisted that there must always be a large live audience who roared its approval.

The three-cornered feed-back effect in the live theatre (and the collective experience of the audience by the audience, even in the cinema) is an important element in the impact of drama. In television and radio the audience may be a much smaller number of people, or even just a solitary individual. But even here a consensus of this kind will develop in a family or group of friends, or alternatively a discussion will result during which contradictory views will be aired. And television drama, because of the much larger total numbers of its audience, can ultimately lead to a similar, if delayed, consensus as that which an audience in the theatre instantly establishes and feels: simply because the many millions of people who have seen a play will talk about it during the following days. A good example was the British television play *Cathy Come Home* which dealt with the plight of the homeless in a powerful semi-documentary style and had very far-reaching consequences on the government's housing policy. In the live theatre such effects are more concentrated and immediately perceptible. At its best, when a fine play in a fine performance coincides with a receptive audience in the theatre, this can produce a concentration of thought and emotion which leads to an enhanced degree of lucidity, of emotional intensity that amounts to a higher level of spiritual insight and can make such an experience akin to a religious one, a memorable high-point in an individual's life.

And, of course, historically drama and religion are very closely linked; they have a common root in religious ritual. What is the nature of ritual and what links ritual

Drama as collective experience: ritual

and drama? Both are *collective* experiences with the three-cornered reinforcement of feed-back from performer to audience, from audience to audience. Man, as a social animal, an animal unable to live in isolation, compelled to form part of a tribe, a clan, a nation, is deeply dependent on such collective experiences. For the identity of a social group consists, by definition, of a common stock of customs, beliefs, concepts, of its language, its myths, its laws, its rules of conduct. But above all, the group—and each individual in it—must be able to experience its own identity: ritual is one of the means by which a primitive tribe as well as a highly developed society experiences this identity: Red Indians dancing round the totem pole, as well as millions of viewers watching the inauguration of a President or the Queen at the Trooping of the Colour are being made to experience directly and overwhelmingly what binds them together as social groups. And all ritual is basically dramatic simply because it combines a spectacle, something to be seen or heard, with a live audience: think of the Eucharist, or a Coronation, or a state funeral.

One can therefore look at ritual as a dramatic, a theatrical event—and one can look at drama as ritual. The dramatic side of ritual manifests itself in the fact that all ritual has a mimetic aspect; it contains an action of a highly symbolic, metaphorical nature, whether this is the dance by which the tribe represents the movements of its totem animal or the breaking of bread and drinking of wine in the Christian Eucharist, or whether, as in West Indian Voodoo or in Asiatic Shamanistic religions, the priest, or indeed members of the congregation, become possessed by the gods and act and speak like them. In many religious rituals the action is, for the faithful, both symbolic and real, in the sense that, for example, the

27

bread and the wine are both symbols of the body of Christ and at the same time the real body of Christ. This also is a truly dramatic aspect of ritual: drama, unlike epic poetry, is an eternal present. Each time *Hamlet* is acted, Hamlet is present and goes through the sequence of the events that happened to him as if they were happening now for the first time. The same is true of ritual. Ritual abolishes time by putting its congregation in touch with events and concepts which are eternal and therefore infinitely repeatable.

And in ritual as in drama the aim is an enhanced level of consciousness, a memorable insight into the nature of existence, a renewal of strength in the individual to face the world. In dramatic terms: catharsis; in religious terms: communion, enlightenment, illumination.

The technical means by which these high spiritual objectives are achieved must of necessity be similar: the use of heightened language or verse, song, music, rhythmical chanting, spectacular visual effects: costume, masks, dance, spectacular architecture. Theatres can be described as secular cathedrals, cathedrals as religious stages. And again and again theatre has come out of ritual, notably in Greece, but also in the European Middle Ages in the miracle plays and mysteries which were a direct extension of religious ritual.

The development of society and of culture is a process of constant differentiation: in ritual we have the common root of music, dance, poetry and drama; in the subsequent process of further differentiation, drama developed into spoken drama, ballet, opera, musical comedy. And spoken drama subdivided itself into the various genres, tragedy, comedy, tragi-comedy, farce and, with later technological development, into the different media of stage, television, radio drama and cinema. Yet from the same root of ritual also stems a great deal of modern political ceremonial—the inauguration of presidents, much of the ritual of great sporting events such as international football or cricket matches or the Olympic Games, processions of all kinds, both religious and secular, and a multitude of other public rituals. All of them still retain many theatrical elements and there are signs that they might again merge with theatre. For example, the modern tendency towards the Happening, staged events involving the audience directly in action, imports theatrical elements into what otherwise might be regarded as a public ritual of another kind, like a masked ball or a banquet.

It is important to keep these facts in mind when talking or thinking about drama. They remind one of the very basic nature of the dramatic and that it pervades practically all manifestations of social life.

In ritual as in the theatre a human community directly experiences its own identity and reaffirms it. This makes theatre an extremely political, because pre-eminently social, form of art. And it is of the very essence of ritual that it not only provides its congregation (or in theatrical terms, its audience) with a collective experience on a high spiritual level, but also in very practical terms teaches them, or reminds them of, its codes of conduct, its rules of social coexistence. All drama is therefore a political event: it either reasserts or undermines the code of conduct of a given society. Playwrights like Ibsen or Shaw attacked the social codes of their society; conventional drawing-room comedy probably reaffirmed the social code of the upper classes that formed its audience. This political aspect of theatre is underlined by the fact that most modern, developed nations have their national theatre (an institution which makes an important contri-

29

bution to each nation's image of itself and defines it in relation to its neighbours) and, indeed, their national play which is performed at important occasions as a kind of ritual reaffirmation of nationhood. The Germans have Goethe's *Faust*, the French have Molière and Racine, and the English Shakespeare. When the Irish nationalist movement got into its stride in the last century, Yeats and Lady Gregory founded the Abbey Theatre with the express purpose of producing such an identity-defining national theatre and national drama. The English national play which perhaps comes nearest to a ritual reaffirmation of English nationhood is, I believe, *Henry V*. It is no coincidence that at the height of the Second World War, when the reaffirmation of the nation's identity and its determination to survive were most urgent, Laurence Olivier produced the film of *Henry V*. The King's great speech at Agincourt constitutes what amounts to the centrepiece of English national ritual;

> This day is call'd the Feast of Crispian:
> He that outlives this day, and comes safe home,
> Will stand a tip-toe when this day is named,
> And rouse him at the name of Crispian.
> He that shall live this day, and see old age,
> Will yearly on the vigil feast his neighbours,
> And say: 'Tomorrow is Saint Crispian:
> Then will he strip his sleeve and show his scars,
> And say, 'These wounds I had on Crispin's Day.'
> Old men forget; yet all shall be forgot,
> But he'll remember with advantages
> What feats he did that day: then shall our names,
> Familiar in his mouth as household words,—
> Harry the King, Bedford and Exeter,
> Warwick and Talbot, Salisbury and Gloster,—

Be in their flowing cups freshly remember'd.
This story shall the good man teach his son;
And Crispin Crispian shall ne'er go by,
From this day to the ending of the world,
But we in it shall be remembered,—
We few, we happy few, we band of brothers;
For he today that sheds his blood with me
Shall be my brother; be he ne'er so vile,
This day shall gentle his condition.
And gentlemen in England now a-bed
Shall think themselves accurs't they were not here;
And hold their manhoods cheap whiles any speaks
That fought with us upon Saint Crispin's day.

I have no doubt whatever that this speech has in the last three centuries played a very important part indeed in forming the cohesion of England as a nation. It is interesting moreover that the speech itself describes how by the handing down of the story of a great battle (and drama is one of the most potent methods by which such a story can be made to live on) the self-image, the martial tradition of a nation is created and enhanced and preserved. Shakespeare's historical plays have had a very important part in defining the identity of England and are thus political realities of the highest order. Even though in Britain's present post-imperial period the attitudes of some circles towards the patriotic glories of the past is changing, this I believe is still the case today.

The performance of a play like *Henry V* inevitably becomes a national ritual. In seeing how his fellow members of the audience respond, each individual spectator can gauge to what extent the national self-image portrayed in the play is still valid. Likewise, changes in a nation's mood will become visible through drama. When

31

Henry V no longer arouses the emotion it intends to arouse, it will be evident that the mood, the ideals, the identity image of the nation have decisively changed. This makes drama a very potent indicator and instrument of political change. In Czechoslovakia, for example, in the years that preceded the Prague Spring of 1968 the theatre played a very important part in showing to the nation that the mood had changed. Each individual, however sceptical he might have become of the party's actions, had no means of knowing what others felt in a society where everyone is careful not to expose himself to political persecution by open criticism of the government. In the theatre, however, the very way in which the audience did or did not respond to political exhortation made the situation clear to everyone. I remember when I was in Prague at the time the feeling of relief and exaltation which swept through the audience at a performance of *Romeo and Juliet* when Mercutio died cursing, A plague on both your houses! Every member of the audience felt the political implication of this condemnation of the useless violence of inter-party conflict and as each individual realised that his neighbour had reacted in the same way the spark of mutual recognition fired.

The French Revolution is sometimes said to have really started at the first performance of Beaumarchais' *Marriage of Figaro*, simply because the way the audience reacted to a highly critical view of the life-style of the aristocracy showed how general anti-aristocratic sentiments had become. This may be a legend or an oversimplification. But it contains a grain of important truth.

4 Style and character

Drama is the most social of the art forms: it is, by its very nature, a collective creation: the playwright, the actors, the designer, the costume-maker, the provider of props, the lighting engineer all contribute, and so does the audience by its very presence. The literary part of drama, the script, is fixed, a permanent entity, but each performance of each production of that text is different, because the actors react differently to different audiences, and of course to their own moods.

This fusion of a fixed and a fluid component is one of the prime advantages of live theatre over the mechanically recorded types of drama—the cinema, the radio play, the television play. By permanently fixing the performance as well as the text these media condemn their products to an inevitable process of obsolescence, simply because styles of acting, dress and make-up, as well as the techniques of recording, change, so that recordings of ancient radio plays or old films bear the hallmarks of the quaint and slightly ridiculous products of another epoch. Only the greatest classics, like Marcel Carné's *Les enfants du paradis,* or Charlie Chaplin's or Buster Keaton's comedies, can perhaps survive such an air of outdatedness.

The most important component of any dramatic performance is the actor. He is the word transformed into living flesh. And flesh in the most tangible meaning of the term. People go to the theatre, above all, to see beautiful people; among other things, actors are also people who exhibit themselves for money.

To deny a powerful erotic component in any dramatic experience would be foolish hypocrisy. Indeed, one of the theatre's—and all other drama's—greatest claims is that it operates at the same time on all levels, from the most basic to the most sublime, and that in the best drama the two achieve perfect fusion. We enjoy Shakespeare's poetry in a play like *Romeo and Juliet* not only because it is supreme poetry but also because that poetry is embodied by a beautiful young woman or man who arouses our desire; the desire enhances the poetry and the poetry ennobles the desire and thus the division between body and mind, the earthy and spiritual—which, in any case, is a false dichotomy—is abolished and the unified nature of man, animal *and* spiritual, reaffirmed.

The actors embody and interpret the text provided by the author. And it would seem that they are entirely free to do this in any manner they like. But that is true only up to a point. For the author has at his disposal a very powerful instrument for imposing on the actors the manner of interpretation he desires. That instrument is style.

Let us assume an actor has to speak the following lines in a play:

Tell me, dear friend, what news you have to bring!
I am all ears, though tossed twixt hope and fear
And yet resolved to bear it be what may...

Or that he has to express the identical idea and situation like this:

Come on, Peter, let's have it. I'm dying to hear the
news...Do sit down...will you have a drink?...you
know how much depends on it for me...I want to be
optimistic about the outcome...yet I've always had my
doubts too. Do you take water or soda?...Look, tell me
what you have to say...I can take it...

Clearly, the first passage, being in verse, in a slightly
elevated language, cannot be acted with the fussiness, the
naturalism of the second passage which expresses the
identical thought and circumstances. By couching the
passage in verse the author has made it impossible, for
example, for the actor to accompany the action by
offering his visitor a drink: one simply doesn't ask
whether the visitor takes water or soda in solemn blank
verse (or if one did it would have a distinctly comic effect
which in this case is obviously not intended). The passage
in elevated poetic language will thus clearly have to be
spoken while the actor maintains a far more dignified,
rigid stance; his gestures will have to be infinitely more
stylised, his features far more still. For an actor speaking
language like this it is, for example, quite unthinkable
that he would scratch his head or pick his nose while
uttering the words. For an actor speaking the second
passage all this would be quite possible; the rhythms are
less formalised, more broken, the words used are more
ordinary. Brecht, a playwright who was also a superb
director in the theatre, demanded that the dramatist
should use gestural language, which means that he should
write in a way which imposes the right style of movement
and action on the actor, compelling him to conform to the
playwright's idea of how the words should be acted.

But the style of writing fulfils another function as
well: an informational function towards the audience.

By the style in which a play is written the audience is instantly, and largely subconsciously, being made aware of how they are to take the play, what to expect from it, on what level they ought to react to it. For the audience's reaction is greatly dependent on their expectations. If they are under the impression that the play is *meant* to be funny they will be more readily inclined to laugh than if they know from the beginning that it is to be taken with deep seriousness. Some of this is communicated to the audience by the title, the author, the actors in the play, or whether on the programme it is described as a tragedy or a farce. Nevertheless there may be many in the audience who do not have this advance information, nor is it always clear, even from the programme, what the dramatist or director intends. At the first performance of Beckett's *Waiting for Godot*, a play in a style highly unusual at the time, the audience did not know how to react, whether to laugh or to cry. But in most cases—in established conventions—the style of speech, of acting, the style of the setting and costumes. instantly conveys the required information to the audience and enables them to pitch their expectation at the desired level: it then tells them, to remain with our example, at what level of abstraction the play will take place. In a tragedy by Racine, for example, the very nature of the highly formalised alexandrines instantly makes it clear that the play will concentrate on the most sublime passions of its characters. In such plays nothing is said about the more petty pre-occupations of the people involved. Phèdre or Andromache are never seen eating, or exchanging small-talk. The verse and the level of the language very soon make us aware of this.

Conversely: what makes a dramatist decide in which style he will write his play? When should he use verse,

Style and character

when prose?

Verse removes the action from the everyday, familiar sphere and makes it clear that no attempt is being made to portray life in all its humdrum pettiness. T.S. Eliot felt that at their climaxes, his plays should reach an intensity of emotion which could only be expressed by the richer language and the rhythmic flow of poetry. In order to enable himself to reach these climaxes by a gentle transition and without a break in style he started a play like *The Cocktail Party* in verse, but verse pitched at so low a level that it almost sounded like prose—

ALEX: You've missed the point completely, Julia:
There were no tigers. That was the point.
JULIA: Then what were you doing, up in a tree?
You and the Maharaja?
ALEX: My dear Julia!
It's perfectly hopeless. You haven't been
listening...

The audience may at this point barely notice that this rather trivial conversation is in verse, but gradually they become aware of its rhythm. At the climax of the play, when one of the characters has suffered martyrdom for her religion, the author can raise the level of emotion and poetry to a much higher level:

REILLY: I'd say that she suffered all that we should
suffer
In fear and pain and loathing—all these
together
And reluctance of the body to become a *thing*.
I'd say she suffered more, because more
conscious
Than the rest of us. She paid the highest price

37

In suffering. That is part of the design.

Another reason why a playwright may choose to put his play in verse is that he is unable to reproduce the actual way people would have spoken in his play, because it takes place in a distant past or in a country or civilisation too remote from us in space to be easily reproduceable in everyday English. Verse removes the necessity of having to try and achieve a completely convincing realistic effect. That is why modern plays dealing with history or exotic locations often tend to be in verse. On the other hand, an author like Bernard Shaw, wanting to emphasise how wrong it was to think of historical characters as different from ourselves, made Joan of Arc or Caesar talk contemporary English, with all the anachronisms this implied; he demythologised these historical characters.

This shows that the level of language, the style in which a play is written—and consequently acted—has something to do with the level at which the audience looks at the characters. The distinguished Canadian critic Northrop Frye has pointed to four levels of discourse— and these apply to the novel as well as to drama: if the audience is to look at the characters as infinitely above them, as gods, we are in the realm of myth; if the audience is to look up to them as men high above them, we are in the realm of the heroic; if the audience is to look at the characters as being on the same level as themselves, we are in a realistic style; and if the audience looks down on the characters as contemptible, this is the ironic mode.

Myths—like Greek tragedy—will require the highest flights of poetic language. Heroic plays about kings and queens and almost superhuman men and women will still need an elevated language.

On the realistic level, when the author confronts us

with people inhabiting the same social level as ourselves, prose is indicated. And if we look down on the characters, if we are meant to feel superior to them in intelligence—for example in farce or satire—the language can again be stylised, because we are again looking at people removed from ourselves, even though that distance is a distance beneath us: the language there can be mechanically repetitive or exaggeratedly silly or indeed mock-verse, as in satires and parodies.

What applies to the general style of the play as a whole is also true of each character: in a good play by an accomplished playwright each character will have his own style of speaking—which will, however, have to be a variable within the overall level of language of the play as a whole.

In other words: having set himself a lower and an upper limit within which the language of the play will move, the author can vary the level inside that range, according to the way he wants us to look at the character or indeed the scene. In moments when he is reflecting on his own deep emotion Hamlet speaks in verse; when instructing the players or relaxed in Ophelia's lap he speaks in prose. And the gravediggers—clowns to whom we, the audience, are to feel superior—speak an even lower, more grotesque prose. When prose is used for lofty sentiments it will be a poetic prose.

Yet language is far from being the only instrument of characterisation at the playwright's disposal. It sets the general mood. The characterisation of the individual people in a play is largely a matter of their action and reaction. One of the most frequent mistakes made by aspiring and inexperienced playwrights is the idea that one can characterise someone in a play by having others talk about him—

JONES: And what do you think of Smith?

MAC: Oh he's mean. Never lends you money even if he's loaded with it.

And so on. One might think that this does characterise Smith. The curious fact—and only long experience convinces one of it—is that in drama this kind of reported characterisation simply does not work. Shakespeare uses descriptions of one character by another one, but the real impact of the characterisation always comes from what the characters themselves do. If you bring Smith on and make him act out his meanness it will have a much greater impact:

JONES: Hey, Smith. You look happy today.

SMITH: I am happy. I've just won fifty pounds at the races. Backed the outsider at 50 to 1.

JONES: Congratulations. By the way—I'm in a jam. Could you lend me five pounds till next Thursday?

SMITH: Sorry, old man. Quite impossible. You know how poor I am....

This has the added advantage that it also characterises the second character as an opportunist who instantly takes a chance. Admittedly this is an oversimplified example, but it does, I think, make the point. Analyse any skilfully written play and you will find that invariably the characterisation is in the action. In drama, of course, language very often *is* action. One could go further and claim that all language in drama of necessity *becomes* action. In drama we are concerned not only with *what* a character says—the purely semantic meaning of their words but with what the character *does* with his words.

40

JIM: Liz, will you come to the pictures with me tomorrow night? There's a Judy Garland movie at the local.

LIZ: Sorry, Jim, I have to wash my hair tomorrow night. Sorry.

What matters is not what the girl says—that she has to wash her hair—but what this line of dialogue *does* to the other character. By using that statement she is rejecting the advances of the young man. That is why actors and critics speak of a text and of a subtext.

This brings me back to the all-important element which constitutes the peculiar power and impact of drama: even in the very simplified little dialogue of my example it is up to the audience to decide for themselves what the action behind the humdrum statement about the girl who has to wash her hair every Thursday night actually was. We, the audience, have to decide whether these words amount to a rejection, and we have to try to decide it on the basis of our own experience, our own reaction to a similar situation in our own lives. Because we have to make this decision we are forced to put ourselves into the shoes of the character who rejects, or the one who is rejected, we have to develop a high degree of empathy, of identification—we experience the action on the stage with the characters. And that action is behind the words, unspoken. What is *not* said is as important in drama—both as action and as characterisation—as what *is* said. It is not the words that matter but the situation in which the words are uttered. In Chekhov's *Cherry Orchard*, in the last act, a situation is contrived in which we all expect that Lopakhin will propose to Varya. Finally the two are brought together in front of us. They exchange the most insignificant small-talk. The words are trivial, but the emotion is tremendous, simply because we are aware of what is happening rather than of what is being said. And what is happening is that these two people are missing their last chance of happiness. Through timidity. Through cowardice. Through an inability to say the right word. Here the absence of language is both powerful and unforgettable characterisation and equally powerful and unforgettable action.

5 *The structure of drama*

Put in its simplest and most mundane terms, the basic task of anyone concerned with presenting any kind of drama to any audience consists in capturing their attention and holding it as long as required. Only when that fundamental objective has been achieved can the more lofty and ambitious intentions be fulfilled: the imparting of wisdom and insight, poetry and beauty, amusement and relaxation, illumination and purging of emotion. If you lose their attention, if you fail to make them concentrate on what is happening, on what is being said, all is lost.

The creation of interest and suspense (in their very widest sense) thus underlies all dramatic construction. Expectations must be aroused, but never, until the last curtain, wholly fulfilled; the action must seem to be getting nearer to the objective yet never reach it entirely before the end; and, above all, there must be constant variation of pace and rhythm, monotony of any kind being certain to lull the attention and induce boredom and somnolence.

Interest and suspense need not necessarily be aroused merely by devices of plot: at the opening of a plotless ballet the beauty of the principal dancers may suffice to

43

arouse interest, and the audience's expectation of seeing the full gamut of steps provides sufficient suspense to sustain concentration for a long while. The statement of a theme, its first variation, and the author's ingenuity in continuing to vary it (provided the theme was in itself attractive enough to arouse interest) might provide sufficient expectation and thus suspense. In Beckett's *Waiting for Godot* the very fact that the characters keep reassuring themselves that nothing ever happens and that there is nothing for them to do creates its own kind of suspense: the audience cannot quite believe that this is so and wants to know what *is* going to happen next. And on the way to their final recognition that, ultimately, there has really not been anything happening, enough interesting episodes have occurred, each of which generated its own interest and suspense.

And there are many kinds of suspense: suspense may lie in a question like, 'What is going to happen next?', but equally well in a question like, 'I know what is going to happen, but *how* is it going to happen?' or, indeed, 'I know *what* is going to happen and I know *how* it is going to happen, but how is X going to react to it?'; or it may be of a quite different type, such as, 'What is it that I see happening?' or 'These events seem to have a pattern;

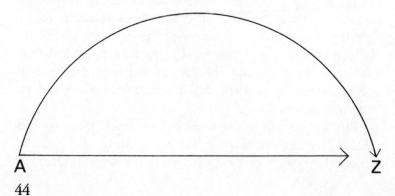

A →   ↓ Z

what kind of pattern will it turn out to be?' One thing, however, is certain: some sort of basic question must emerge fairly early in any dramatic form so that the audience can, as it were, settle down to its main element of suspense. One might say that the major theme of the play must become clear in good time. In most plays or films it is a question, such as who committed the murder, whether the boy will get the girl in the end, or the deceived husband find out about his wife's lover. Once the audience has grasped this main theme, this main objective of the action, their expectation is firmly fixed on the final point and they know where they and the play are going, what its principal *question* is. Their attention is firmly pointed in the right direction. The only question is, by what circuitous route, by which arc will the final answer be reached?

Yet the human attention span is relatively short. One major suspense element is not enough to hold an audience's attention throughout the course of a complete play. On that main arc, subsidiary arcs, arising from the arousal of subsidiary suspense elements must be superimposed. While our main interest is held by the question of who committed the murder, we are, at the

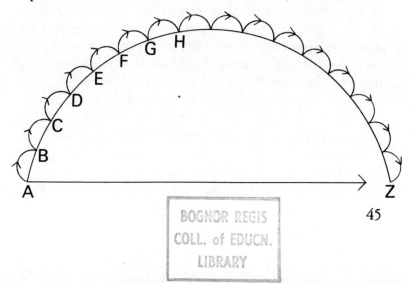

same time, and in a much shorter time span, eagerly asking ourselves whether the gardener who is being questioned at this moment actually saw the murderer jump over the wall, etc. The main suspense element carries the subsidiary one on its back, as it were. And of course, subsidiary suspense elements may precede the emergence of the main theme or objective of the play. In *Hamlet*, for example, the first suspense element is a relatively minor one: will the ghost appear again? Then: will he appear to Hamlet? Then, when he has appeared: what will he say? And it is only after Hamlet and we have heard what the Ghost has to say that the main revenge theme of the play and the main suspense element emerges: will Hamlet succeed in his revenge. Only then do we realise the nature of the main arc on which the minor suspense elements that kept us concentrating on the action had been supported.

There is thus an element of suspense needed for each scene or section of the action, superimposed on the main objective or suspense momentum of the whole play. At any given moment in a play the director and the actors must be aware of these major—strategical—and minor— i.e. tactical, within the scene—objectives which coexist and mutually support each other. Yet there is a third, purely local, microscomic element of suspense at any given moment in a well-devised play,—the micro-suspense of the line of dialogue or single detail of business the actors are engaged in at that moment. The suspense of the main action depends on the existence of at least two solutions to the main problem of the play: will the murderer be found or not; will boy get girl or not. The suspense of each scene must, analogously, depend on at least two possible outcomes of that scene's objective: will the ghost appear or not; will he speak or not. The suspense in the smallest units of dialogue or business must consist, accordingly, in several possible answers to each question or statement made in the dialogue, or indeed in the stage business and gestures that make up the scene. Predictability is the death of suspense and therefore of drama. Good dialogue is unpredictable. Lines that elicit only predictable answers, gestures that duplicate what has already been conveyed by other means, are dead and should be eliminated. The brilliance of the dialogue of great comedy writers like Noel Coward or Oscar Wilde lies in its paradox and surprise; the greatness of giants among playwrights like Shakespeare lies in the originality of their language and their images (which is another way of saying their unexpectedness and surprise). The dialogue, which serves the immediate tactical objective of the given scene or segment, thus superimposes a third arc, a third element of suspense:

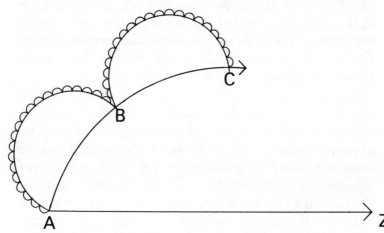

Each surprising formulation, each verbal felicity, each grain of wit or original verbal image, contribute to the interest, the unpredictability, the attention-holding quality of the dialogue. And, of course, in film and television

47

drama the interest and suspense created by the movement of the camera, visual wit and pictorial felicities fulfil exactly the same function; the same is true of the actors' expressions and movements both on the stage and on the screen—a seemingly dead line may become pregnant with suspense through an unexpected glance from one of the actors to another, a gleam which comes into their eyes.

The pattern outlined here is merely schematic. There is no reason why there should not be a multitude of elements of interest and suspense interacting in far more complex patterns. Yet the three basic strands are essential. A cross-section through any dramatic action should, at any given point, yield at least these three. If one of them is missing, or weak, the audience's attention will flag.

The establishment of the main objective of the play is usually called the exposition. This is a useful term although it has now become somewhat obsolete. In the traditional well-made play the exposition provided a firm framework of reference for the relationship of the characters to each other, their previous history as well as the play's principal theme. Contemporary drama, both on the stage and in the mass media, makes far fewer firm commitments of this kind. As mass audiences are exposed to more and more drama, the general level of sophistication is bound to rise: people are becoming more observant, more adept at decoding hints that are dropped, but also more sceptical of taking at its face value what is said or shown. So the level of uncertainty which is permissible in drama has perceptibly risen; indeed, this uncertainty has itself introduced a new factor of suspense. In a film by Antonioni or Altman, just as in a play by Beckett or Ionesco, we may well no longer ask the question which most conventional drama poses for the spectator: what's going to happen next? but the much more general question: what's happening? With this evolution away from the classical exposition, the other traditional terms used in describing the structure of the well-made play have also become somewhat less serviceable. If the exposition is less clear-cut, much of what used to be called the development or complication of the plot tends to merge into a prolonged unravelling of the dramatic strands which might also be called a continued exposition and as a result the traditional turning point (*peripeteia*) and the climax and solution of the play may also be less clear-cut. Nevertheless, these concepts are extremely valuable where they are applicable. One should merely beware of thinking that where they are not applicable there must be something basically wrong with the play. The evocation of interest in the audience is not just, as many would-be playwrights assume, a matter of inventing a suitable story-line, action, plot. The secret lies in the fusion of plot-interest with interest in the characters. Even the most violent action remains without impact and basically uninteresting if the audience does not know, does not like, and is therefore not sufficiently interested in the characters. How do characters become objects of affection or interest? Casting, the personality of the actors chosen to embody them, can help a great deal. But basically it is a matter of that third, purely local element of suspense, the quality of the dialogue they speak. A character who never says a line which is arresting, witty, amusing or interesting, will have great difficulty in catching the audience's sympathy or, conversely, loathing. And then however ingenious the twists of the plot he is involved in, the audience will care little for them.

The awakening and holding of the audience's attention

through expectation, interest and suspense is, as I have stressed, the most primitive and mundane aspect of dramatic structure. The more complex and subtle problems of form rest on this basis. With the exception of radio drama, all other dramatic forms exist both in space (like painting or photography) and in time (like music and poetry). Thus a combination of spatial and temporal elements allows an infinite number of structural permutations between spatial unity in rhythmic diversity on the one hand and unity of pace and tone in a wide variety of visual changes on the other. There can be patterns of intensities rising to a climax and then subsiding, ascending forms of gradual intensification of all elements (speed, pace, rhythm light, colour) and descending ones in which they gradually run down; or again, circular ones in which the end rejoins the shape of the beginning. The repetition of various elements at recurring intervals gives one shape, violent contrasts and abrupt and surprising transitions give another.

The essential truth to remember, however, is that while formlessness is amorphous, without discernible structure, all form, all structure depends on articulation, the joining together of distinct elements. This is important enough in the spatial dimension where the grouping of characters on the stage, the distribution of colour and light, make all the difference between chaos and comprehensibility. In the temporal dimension it is even more vital: just as a piece of music proceeds with its own rhythm and must be subdivided into distinct sections, the verses and chorus of a song, the movements of a sonata or symphony, so the movement of drama in any form must be similarly articulated and shaped. If one sets out on a long walk in a town in which one has just arrived to reach a destination one or two miles down a straight road, the walk at first will appear endless. The second time, when one remembers landmarks on the way which become subsidiary objectives and articulate the journey, the boredom will lessen and the time will pass much more swiftly. For something which is shapeless and contains no indication of its internal articulation could be endless. Once we realise that the distance is divided into—say— four parts, each of which is within easy reach, the terror of setting out towards an undefined, distant goal disappears. Clarity of structure and a clear 'signposting' of the course of the action are thus very important formal elements in the structuring of drama. And the more the variation between each segment and its neighbour, the less will be the danger of monotony, another dangerous source of boredom.

In an art form in which the structuring of the work in a time dimension is of such importance, it is only natural that timing, a sense of timing, is the essential hallmark of the good playwright, as well as of director and actor. This starts with the length (or brevity) of each distinct scene or section of a dramatic work and ends with the tiniest pause that elapses between the raising of an eyebrow and the delivery of a line.

Economy is the essence of timing. Drama is, among many other things, a method of communication. Watching a play, a film, a television serial, listening to a radio play, we have declared our willingness to have something communicated to us and therefore we are intent on decoding the communication: everything that happens in that frame on the screen, on that stage, in that half-hour of broadcasting, must contribute to that act of communication. Max Frisch describes in his diaries how when he was first asked to come to the Zurich theatre to be commissioned to write his first play, he arrived too early

51

and sat waiting in the empty, dark auditorium. Suddenly the lights on the stage went up, a stage-hand appeared and placed some chairs in readiness for the rehearsal that was about to start. Frisch describes how he watched this activity with rapt attention, how suddenly every movement of the man acquired tremendous significance, simply because it was happening on a lit stage, within the picture frame of that stage. For we are conditioned to think of a stage (or a television or cinema screen) as spaces within which significant things are being shown; they therefore concentrate our attention and compel us to try and arrange everything that happens there into a significant pattern, to make sense of it as a pattern. Hence, anything that is unnecessary or does not contribute to that pattern will appear as an intrusion, an irritant. The playwright, the director, the actors, the designer of sets and costumes must therefore constantly be aware of the function of each detail within the whole structure. A line of dialogue may not directly contribute to the movement of the plot, but it may be essential to establish some vital clue to the character; a piece of furniture in the set may never be needed for the action, yet it may be important to establish atmosphere. In *Uncle Vanya* Chekhov specifies that above the desk of that Russian landowner there should hang a large map of Africa. Africa never enters into the play, but the very incongruity of the map's presence illustrates the wayward, ineffectual character of Vanya himself. He must have found that map in an attic, or picked it up cheaply in some antique shop and put it up, perhaps because it reminded him of a world of adventure beyond his reach, or perhaps only to cover a damp patch on that wall. The map of Africa can thus be seen as a brilliant piece of character-drawing on the part of Chekhov—and an extremely economical one at that. Its presence does not lengthen the play by one second, yet it communicates a great deal.

This is not to say that all the many elements of action, dialogue, design or music which a performance uses to communicate with the audience must be consciously apprehended by every member of the audience as part of the total communication he is receiving. Much of the impact of drama is subliminal and instinctive. In real life we react to the appearance and the mode of speech of a new acquaintance instinctively and without consciously analysing each element of the overall impression he makes on us. Similarly in a play we may find the hero sympathetic, the heroine attractive, without the process by which we have arrived at this reaction becoming conscious. But the process of choosing someone who will evoke such an instinctive reaction to play that part must be a conscious and deliberate decision on the part of the director, and the actor thus chosen must in turn make a deliberate effort to portray a sympathetic and attractive character.

The total structure of a dramatic work thus depends on a very delicate balance of a multitude of elements, all of which must contribute to the total pattern and all of which are wholly interdependent. A scene which is very quiet may appear boring after another quietscene: it will come as a welcome relief after a very noisy one. Context is all: in the right context an almost imperceptible gesture may move mountains, the simplest phrase may turn into the most sublime poetic utterance. That is the true miracle of drama, its true poetry.

Yet, while the effects may appear mysterious, the way in which they are achieved can be analysed and understood. Once the spectator's attention and interest have been caught, once he has been induced to follow the action with the utmost concentration and involvement, his powers of perception are heightened, his emotions are freely flowing and he will, in fact, reach a heightened state of consciousness: more receptive, more observant, better able to discern the underlying unity and pattern of human existence. This is what makes true receptivity to any art akin to religious experience (or the heightened awareness of the world induced by certain drugs). And among all artistic experiences of this kind drama is one of the most powerful.

6 The critical vocabulary

In talking about any subject we cannot do without a specialised vocabulary of terms and concepts. This is especially true of drama which is an exceedingly complex art form. In discussing style I pointed out that the form of language employed in the opening scene of a play sets the key, as it were and communicates the spirit in which the whole play is to be taken by the audience. In this context what matters is whether the language is elevated or coarse, in prose or verse, whether the actors' movements are formal or realistic.

Styles of dramatic writing have changed over the centuries, as indeed have the conventions by which audiences have been offered drama (such as the restriction to two and later three actors in Greek tragedy or the rigid confinement of all drama behind the frame of the proscenium arch in the eighteenth and nineteenth centuries). In periods and civilisations with unified, coherent world-view accepted by the vast majority without question—periods like the classical Greek world or the Middle Ages–the arts, and drama in particular, tend to reflect that attitude to life by a single and unified style of presentation. In other periods, like our own, a wide variety of philosophies and attitudes to life coexist and there is a high degree of historical consciousness, an awareness that each epoch, each country is different. In such periods a variety of possible styles and conventions of presentation coexist at the same time and is available to directors, actors, playwrights and designers to be used as they wish, just like the colours on the palette of a painter from which he can choose at will. A present-day director can decide whether he wants to produce a play, say by Shakespeare, in a realistic style or an expressionist one, as a Commedia dell'arte or a formal Renaissance spectacle; he can also decide whether to stage it in the convention of the proscenium arch, or on an open arena stage like the one at Chichester or Stratford, Ontario, or indeed in the round. With all these possibilities available to the artists, no wonder that people whose job it is to offer discourse on drama—the critics who explain, evaluate, criticise it, or (since no collaborative art like drama is possible without communication between its practitioners,) the directors, actors, designers of sets, costumes, and lighting who talk about it among themselves—no wonder all these people need a vocabulary of concepts to establish efficient communication

Hence the need for an elaborate critical vocabulary. Yet it must always be kept in mind that terms like classical, romantic or expressionist, Brechtian or Absurdist were coined for a specific purpose. Their value lies in their power to convey general impressions; they do not denote rigidly defined concepts, categories that can be clearly kept apart in watertight compartments.

A play which has classical features can have romantic and realistic ones as well: the porter's scene in *Macbeth* is coarsely realistic while Macbeth's great speech at the end is highly poetic. The great German playwright Schiller, who made an adaptation of *Macbeth* at the end of the eighteenth century, omitted the porter's scene, one of the most effective in the play, because he felt that it could not possibly remain in a poetic play! This is one example of the grave practical dangers of taking these concepts too seriously—of thinking that there is something deeply illogical, a self-contradiction, in a poetic play which contains a realistic scene and that it is therefore some sort of outrage against nature and good sense to allow them to remain side by side

To quote a more recent example: Harold Pinter developed a certain style of dialogue and plot in his earlier plays. A critic of one of his later plays reproached him for having written something which was not sufficiently Pinteresque, as though he had an obligation to stick to the style he had created. Pinter was rightly indignant about this; for, in effect, the critic had elevated an amusing and perfectly valid adjective, descriptive of a certain approach to writing, into an absolute. Just as an apple always has to be an apple and can't suddenly turn into a pear, he implied, once Pinter had been labelled Pinteresque he was not to be allowed suddenly to write in a different vein. vein.

It may seem silly even to mention such a misunderstanding. But if one looks at the vast 'critical' literature about drama, one soon realises that there are only too many examples of this kind of misuse of terms.

There are two different species of critical terms of this kind: those which were deliberately created as programmatic devices or slogans of groups or schools of playwrights and artists, and those which are merely descriptive and arise out of a necessity to bring order into a wide variety of spontaneously existing features. These descriptive terms are coined *post factum* by critics or academics who have to teach the history of an art form; the artists themselves may never have been aware of the existence of such terms, rather like Molière's Monsieur Jourdain who was very proud to discover that he had been talking prose all his life without knowing it.

An example of a movement which arose gradually out of a wide and impassioned discussion of where literature and drama should be going, but without at first a programmatic formula, is German Romanticism. A desire to react against the rigid rules of French classicism, combined with a nationalist impulse, a revival of interest in the Middle Ages, a Catholic and pietistic religious revival which caused an interest in mysticism and the occult—in short, a number of powerful impulses arising out of a multitude of social and historical forces—combined to create a new approach to literature and drama which eventually was given a theoretical basis and labelled Romanticism. Poets and playwrights like Schiller and Goethe who consciously strove towards a classical ideal, without being fully aware of it, produced many works we now consider typically Romantic. Finally, a number of important critics, like the Schlegel brothers, Tieck, Brentano and others crystallised these tendencies into the philosophy and aesthetics of German Romanticism.

In France the Romantic movement arose later, under the leadership of writers such as Dumas, Gautier and Victor Hugo who, greatly influenced by the German Romantics as well as by the English Lake poets, consciously proclaimed a new aesthetic. So in France Romanticism was a school with its own ideology and objectives.

When I wrote my book on the Theatre of the Absurd I tried to provide some sort of help to critics who, I felt, were missing the point of a number of plays I had greatly enjoyed and admired. I tried to isolate and analyse what the plays of Beckett, Ionesco, Adamov, Genet, Pinter, etc., had in common—features such ,as the absence of a full exposition or solution, a wide use of dreamlike images and situations, a new kind of associative rather than rational logic and so on. Of course, if a journalist, as journalists will, then asked M. Ionesco or M. Adamov whether they were now members of the Absurdist movement these highly individualistic men of genius would indignantly repudiate the suggestion, deny ever having joined such a club, and even assert that they had nothing in common with the supposed other members of that club. And, of course, they would be right. But so was I. If you asked Milton and Webster whether they both belonged to the Baroque period, they would have denied any knowledge of such a label (which, indeed, was applied to the period by critics at a much later date), and Milton would have been very indignant indeed to have been bracketed with the wild and extravagant Webster. Yet to us both are unmistakably the children of the same epoch, using, in very different ways, to very different purposes, the language, concepts and style of the seventeenth century. In other words, a descriptive term applied *post factum* may be useful even if the people to whom it is applied are unaware of its existence and meaning, provided that such a term is not taken as totally defining the works to which it is applied, but merely as descriptive of certain features which they have in common and which are basic to them. Neither a mouse nor an elephant has to know that they are both mammals, and the fact that they are both mammals certainly does not mean that they are identical. And yet the term is of considerable usefulness in understanding both these animals.

The irony is that in those cases, like the French Romantic Movement, in which the artists concerned are determined to put a common ideology into practice, their conscious striving for similar ends often covers up deep unconscious differences; whereas in those 'movements' in which the practitioners are unaware, consciously, of any common endeavour, we often find very deep inner similarities and connections. Brecht's plays, although written in an orthodox Marxist spirit, were for many years not performed in the Soviet Union because they were too highly stylised—'formalist'—and did not comply with the compulsory realist style, which the rulers there proclaimed the only truly Marxist approach to drama.

There is a further pair of critical terms about which there is a great deal of confusion: realism and naturalism. Realism is a descriptive term coined by critics, naturalism was the programmatic slogan of a school.

In the mid-nineteenth century playwrights reacted against the high flown poetic drama of the Romantics and there was a tendency to write in prose about everyday life. We can see that tendency in the earlier works of Henrik Ibsen, who started out writing romantic comedies and vast epic verse dramas (like *Peer Gynt* and *Brand*) but later turned towards social subjects treated in prose.

Naturalism on the other hand was a movement, initiated by Emile Zola, with a well-defined programme of action: the application of the new positivist, scientific spirit of the age to literature. Zola not only wanted a realistic representation of everyday life, he rejected the idea which had infused the classical, the romantic and even the realistic theatre of his period, that art should strive to show the beautiful, heroic, uplifting and inspiring. Zola wanted the artist to uncover the truth about society in the same spirit of objective inquiry as that of a natural scientist's approach to nature. It was in this spirit

60

that Ibsen in *Ghosts* brought a hitherto taboo subject like venereal disease into the theatre and caused an enormous scandal.

The terminology of realism and naturalism haunts our own epoch as well. In the Soviet Union—and through her influence among the committed left throughout the world—the term socialist realism is widely used as the officially approved style of Soviet art. Naturalism, on the other hand, is a term of abuse in Soviet circles. Socialist realism insists on showing Soviet society as it ought to be rather than as it is, while naturalism is the term used to decry works of art which also show the more sordid side of that society.

A knowledge of this particular use of the terms is important, because it tends to lead to endless confusion when introduced into controversy in Western countries about committed art and also because the critical work of a very great playwright like Brecht is incomprehensible without an awareness of the special sense in which the terms appear in his discussion of realism versus formalism. Brecht was accused of not being realistic enough because he liked parables and fantasy, and for many years his works were not performed in the Soviet Union because they were not realistic in the Soviet sense. He argued that they *were* realistic because they gave insights into the real world, the world as it is, regardless of the poetic and anti-illusionist means and devices he used.

But let me return to naturalism as practised by Zola, Ibsen, Strindberg and Gerhart Hauptmann at the turn of the century. The basic impulse behind the naturalistic movement was a determination to capture the whole of human experience, however sordid and ugly, to leave nothing unsaid. It did this by an accumulation of significant detail. In romantic drama, the heroes talked in lofty

61

poetic terms about love or glory; in Ibsen's *The Master Builder* Solness is concerned with his buildings, including the church he is erecting. And when the plot turns on his being challenged as to whether he is still able to climb to the top of the steeple, and he falls, inevitably that steeple becomes a symbol of his ambitions and his inability to live up to them. By concentrating on the concrete detail rather than on abstract sentiments, naturalism tended to transform itself into a style in which objects increasingly became symbols, embodiments of ideas.

So naturalism merged into symbolism. And as the writers concerned concentrated more and more on these symbols, which after all are in the nature of poetic metaphors, lyrical images, so symbolism came full circle and turned into a type of neo-romanticism which again did not disdain the use of verse. The leader of the German naturalist school, Gerhart Hauptmann, best exemplifies this development: he started out with plays depicting the sordid side of life, hereditary alcoholism or the brutish existence of the proletariat, but gradually veered towards historical and poetic subjects in verse.

Strindberg and the German playwright Frank Wedekind, who had both started out as naturalists, took a slightly different path. In their determination to represent experience exactly as it really was they soon discovered that depicting the external world tells only half the story; you also had to include the way that world was experienced by an individual, and that meant his internal world. Hence Strindberg wrote a number of such plays— *The Ghost Sonata, To Damascus* and the *Dream Play* itself which, quite in the spirit of naturalism, tried to depict a dream. Wedekind, on the other hand, experienced the world as a pretty grotesque place: he tended towards savage caricature, but also towards dreams. At the end of his seminal play *Spring Awakening*, which depicts quite naturalistically, the tragedy of its teenage protagonists ruined by their ignorance of sex and which savagely and grotesquely caricatures the desiccated monsters of the teaching staff of the school, the hero is confronted by the ghost of his now dead friend, headless, carrying his head under his arm, as well as by a mysterious stranger in a mask. The first tries to seduce him to commit suicide and the second to persuade him to live on. This goes further than mere symbolism. The writer is trying to embody the essence of the event: the forces struggling for the young hero's soul, his death wish and his desire to live on, are being made explicit. This was the beginning of expressionism, where the emphasis on making the essential nature of the conflict clear, to *express* it as forcefully and directly as possible, dominated. Where naturalism tried to paint a realistic picture by accumulating a wealth of telling, small external detail and thus was essentially impressionistic, this tendency discarded the detail for the sake of maximum expressiveness, hence expressionism.

In expressionist drama the characters frequently do not even have names (in *Ghost Sonata*: the Old man, the Student, the Mummy, the Colonel, etc.).

One of the major influences on the theatre of our time was Bertolt Brecht who, being a man who enjoyed theorising, coined a wealth of fashionable terms. He rejected naturalism as well as the classical and romantic theatre, and ridiculed the high-flown but egocentric idealism of the expressionists, although he took many ideas from them. His favourite term, at least in his earlier and middle years, was 'epic theatre'. Epic in this sense has nothing to do with the concept of the Hollywood epic, meaning a lavishly produced historical film; it is derived

from the classical German period where the leading poets
(Goethe and Schiller), in trying to define their ideas of
drama, talked a great deal about the difference between
the dramatic mode of telling a story as against the
narrative mode, as used in the novel or the long epic
poem. So they spoke of dramatic as against epic poetry.
Epic (narrative) poetry, which includes the novel, novella
and short story, presents the events as having happened
in the past, there and then. Dramatic poetry, they said,
presents events as though they were happening here and
now, an eternal present. The playwright and the actors
must strive to make the audience think they are present at
the events they see, and the actors should actually believe
that they are Hamlet or Othello, so that the audience,
wholly concentrating on their actions, will forget that
they are watching a fiction and take it as something they
are witnessing or even living through. Brecht thought
that this was in contradiction to the Marxist view of
history, which postulates that each epoch, having different social conditions produces different ways of feeling or
consciousness. If a spectator in 1950 thought that the
events he saw in a performance of *Oedipus* could have
happened in this century, if he should at the end say: ' I
felt exactly what poor Oedipus felt', then such a spectator
would be convinced of the existence of something like an
unchangeable human nature—a deeply anti-Marxist
concept, for the whole aim of Marx was to change human
nature by improving social conditions. So Brecht wanted
an 'undramatic'–an epic–theatre, which did not pretend
that the events of the play were happening here and now
but made it clear that the actors were merely demonstrat-
ing social conditions of other epochs in order to impart
important information to the audience, which should
watch the play in a detached, critical frame of mind. This

is the famous *Verfremdungseffekt*, often wrongly trans-
lated as alienation effect. It really means strange-making
effect—in other words, a method by which the spectator
is kept detached from the action, safe against the temptation of being sucked into it.

Brecht's theatre therefore is anti-illusionist: that is, no
effort is made to create an illusion of reality. Instead the
stage becomes something of a lecture platform, a laboratory in which models of human behaviour are examined,
tested and evaluated. But, of course, Brecht was also a very
great poet. That fact rather than his theories, fascinating
and stimulating though they are, is the secret of his
success as a playwright.

And finally the Theatre of the Absurd or Absurdist
theatre. Whereas the naturalists and Brecht concentrate
on social reality, the external world, other playwrights,
following Strindberg and also novelists of dream states
like Kafka and Joyce, turned towards the representation
of the world of fantasy and dream. In Ionesco's *Amédée*,
for example, a married couple is terrified because in the
next room there is a corpse, perhaps that of the wife's
lover killed by the husband, and that corpse keeps
growing...an absurd concept, a growing corpse, but
terrifying. It grows so large that finally a huge foot breaks
through the door and as it keeps growing gradually
pushes the couple out of their house...a real nightmare
but also a powerful image which, on reflection, makes
sense. Whatever happened in the next room, the love of
the couple died there. And a dead love does indeed grow:
it gets more and more unbearable and finally breaks up
the marriage and the home. So in plays such as these, the
nightmare or dream images also become poetic metaphors of reality. Brecht's theatre strives towards the epic
mode of poetry, the absurdist theatre tends towards the

65

lyrical mode. Just as a poem is sometimes a pattern of
unfolding images, metaphors and similes, an absurdist
play uses concretised poetic images which gradually
unfold and disclose their deeper meaning. In the conventional realistic play, the main emphasis is on plot and
character; in the Brechtian epic play it is on the demonstration of human behaviour patterns; in the absurdist
play the main means of conveying significance and effect
are image and metaphor. Even more basic than these
terms in the critical vocabulary of contemporary theatre,
however, is another group of concepts—the genres of
tragedy, comedy, tragi-comedy and farce.

7 *Tragedy, comedy, tragicomedy*

The most frequently used terms in the critical vocabulary of drama are those denoting the different genres–above all the two basic genres: tragedy and comedy. An immense amount of speculation and philosophising exists on this subject and these theoretical concepts have exercised a profound influence on the actual practice of playwriting, acting and production. And yet, most curiously, there is no consensus about it all, no generally accepted and acceptable definition of either tragedy or comedy, let alone of the many intermediate genres like comedy of manners, farce, tragi-comedy, burlesque, domestic comedy, domestic tragedy, melodrama and so on.

Of course, the simplest definition, one which many theoreticians would call no more than simple-minded, is still generally applicable, although it resolves very little: a play with a sad ending is a tragedy, a play with a happy ending a comedy. That seems to be the criterion by which Shakespeare's friends arranged his plays in the First Folio: his *Measure for Measure,* for instance, a play containing many dark and brooding events and on the whole far from funny or even lighthearted, appears among the Comedies, simply because it has an ending without any corpses; the same applies to *The Winter's*

Tale which modern critics classify among Shakespeare's Romances. Because it has a forgiving conciliatory ending, it also appears among the Comedies. On the other hand, Shakespeare's editors had the whole category of Histories—which are not tragedies, although violent deaths abound in them. They are certainly not comedies either, although they do contain some funny and light-hearted scenes, like those in which Falstaff appears in *Henry IV*. What then are they? The term 'history play' deals with subject matter rather than genre.

It is easy see some of the problems this theory of genres creates even at the most basic levels. Each period of history has had its own prevailing views which at times hardened into rigid rules; these then often became straitjackets. Under the influence of French classical drama it was regarded as axiomatic that tragedy had to have leading characters who must be members of royalty, on the assumption that only people of such high rank could have sentiments noble enough to comply with the high requirements of the genre. When, in the eighteenth century, plays were written with a sad ending and with leading characters from the middle classes, this was felt to be quite a revolution and the term 'bourgeois tragedy' or 'domestic tragedy' was coined to distinguish these lowly plays from the traditional high tragedy. As a critic I am, of course, fascinated by the difficult problems of the definition of the genres and their aesthetic and philosophical implications. But as a practitioner of drama, a working director, I look at them from a completely different angle. This is not to say that, even from this practical point of view, I think the definition of the genres is unimportant. Quite the contrary. But that importance is practical rather than theoretical. As a director one has to make a decision about the genre to which the play one tackles should belong. Not from some abstract principle, but simply from the point of view of how it is to be acted. Indeed, it is quite possible to act a play as either comedy or tragedy.

This is the problem which besets all directors who try their hand at Chekhov. Chekhov himself said about *The Cherry Orchard*: 'I call the play comedy', while his director Stanislavsky wrote to him: 'this is not a comedy or a farce, as you wrote, it is a tragedy, whatever the solution you may have found for the better life in the last act.' Thus a play like *The Cherry Orchard* can be treated as comedy or as tragedy. The way in which Mme Ranevskaya loses her property through sheer incompetence and indecisiveness can be shown to be silly and therefore funny, something to be looked down upon by the audience who must feel superior to all that bungling, laziness and lack of willpower; but one could—and often does—produce the play as a deeply sad account of the downfall of the last truly civilised people in a society which is being engulfed by commercialism, vulgarity and mass barbarism.

Whether the director sees such a play as tragedy, comedy or even farce will have an immediate and very practical effect on his handling of the production: it will influence his casting, the design of the set and costumes, the tone, rhythm and pacing of the performance. And, above all, the style in which it is to be acted.

Let me illustrate this by a simple example. Here is a brief dialogue which, in itself, might be part of a tragedy, a comedy or a farce. In the text itself there is nothing to indicate which of the three it is:

SHE: What has happened? Are you hurt, my darling?
HE: Oh, it's nothing. I slipped...

SHE: But you are...bleeding...there is blood on
your...nose—
HE: I slipped...I must have broken my leg...
SHE: It looks worse than that...I'm afraid...

Imagine how this text would be acted if it formed part of a
tragedy, if, for example, the wound was really a serious
one and this dialogue preceded a scene in which the man
died. Read it aloud in that manner. The actors—in this
case you—would have to bring out real anxiety, fear, the
gradual dawning of the seriousness of the situation. The
man would have to try and play down the seriousness of
the wound and make a brave effort to laugh it off, yet
underneath that there would be his own anxiety and fear
of death, and so on. The actors would have to develop a
very high degree of empathy, of identification with the
characters; they would have to make an immense effort to
reach the highest possible pitch of emotion. As a result
the timing of the scene would be slow, the pauses
indicated by dots would be long and pregnant.

Now imagine the same five lines in the context of a
light character comedy, a gently amusing play in which
perhaps a scene like this, by revealing the girl's deeper
interest in the young man, might set off a romance
between them. It would soon turn out that the wound was
not serious, but the girl's anxiety would have shown how
fond she is of the young man. The way the actors would
have to attack the scene would then be quite different; far
more playful, more detached, with more emphasis on
elegance of expression, lightness of touch, urbane manners. Even the way the actors use their voices would be
different. Instead of heavy, emotional chest-tones, the
lines could now come from a higher register. The pauses
would probably be less pregnant and therefore shorter.

There would still have to be genuine feeling and compassion in the delivery, but compassion in a far lighter, more playful vein.

And now try to read the same five lines as they would be acted in a farce, let us say during the pursuit of the lover by the husband: the lover has jumped from the bedroom window and is found by his mistress. The delivery of the lines will be very fast, breathless, in a falsetto voice; they will sound caricatured, mechanical, grotesque. Instead of coming out of real anxiety, a line like 'there is blood...on your...nose' will appear as a grotesquely hysterical shriek. This is the cruel laughter that greets the man who has slipped on a banana skin. The French philosopher Henri Bergson identified the source of laughter as the experience of seeing a human being treated or acting as a mechanism. Farce does just that: in farce events develop with the relentless mechanical precision of a machine and the characters appear as mere cogs. Charlie Chaplin being fed on the conveyor belt by a feeding machine in *Modern Times* and Buster Keaton on an ocean liner trying to cook an egg in the vast cauldron designed to cook for thousands are classical embodiments of this concept.

In Chapter 4 I mentioned Northrop Frye's division of literary modes by the relation between the audience and the characters. In a heroic and a mythical world the audience looks up to the characters as gods or great men; in a realistic mode they are seeing themselves on a level with them; in an ironic mode they feel superior to them, look down on them with contempt or derision. Now clearly the characters of tragedy are gods or heroes, and are looked up to; the characters of realistic drama—and that includes all comedy—are seen as on a level with the audience. In farce they are definitely looked down upon by

71

the audience—but not only by the audience: by the actors too.

One can also approach this question from the psychological angle—the degree of identification. If a character on the stage loses his trousers and I identify with him (that is, if the actors and the production have compelled me to look at the action from that character's point of view), then I shall be embarrassed by his experience, I shall feel as embarrassed as he does.

I don't think a character in tragedy would ever lose his trousers, but in a gentle, realistic comedy the embarrassment may well be experienced. If I do not identify with the character who loses his trousers, if the style of production and writing has made it clear to me that I am supposed to regard the character as a stupid ninny to whom I am superior, at whom I am looking from the outside rather than the inside, then I shall laugh out loud when I see him lose his trousers, when I see him embarrassed and humiliated.

Freud, another important writer on the nature of laughter, thought that laughter was caused by the relief of anxiety: what shakes us when we laugh is the nervous energy released when we realise that the misfortune we saw coming does not directly affect us, that we are free from its consequences. In a tragic scene, or a comedy scene which causes us anxiety, this anxiety is either not relieved at all and we suffer with the characters (in tragedy) or it is only partially relieved and we smile in sympathy with them (in comedy). In farce we laugh out loud as the cream cake hits Stan Laurel, because we are made to feel that we would never be in such a situation, it could only happen to a clown like that, which is not to say that there isn't much more to the Laurel and Hardy comedies.

Tragedy, comedy, tragi-comedy

The relief from anxiety which plays such an important part in comic drama—both comedy and farce, each in its own style—can be clearly seen in a great classical comedy like Moliere's *Tartuffe*. We laugh about the way in which Tartuffe deceives and wheedles Orgon, because we feel superior to Orgon. Why? Because very cunningly the author makes Orgon blind to Tartuffe's hypocrisy while we, the audience, see it all too clearly. This is one of the basic devices of all drama: the audience is made to know more than the character on the stage. Or, indeed, less. If they know less than the characters, there is suspense, tension, expectation; if they know more they become deeply involved, they almost want to cry out to the characters not to act so foolishly. That is the source of a great deal of comedy. It is also the reason why *Tartuffe* for most of its action is seen as funny by the audience, although what is being shown is a sad thing, the ruin of a good man and a happy family. Yet, towards the end of the play, when it becomes clear that Orgon's ruin is indeed almost completed, the audience's anxiety and compassion are aroused and they do feel sorry and uncomfortable. It is at this moment that the appearance of the King's envoy suddenly and dramatically relieves the tension, releases the audience's laughter and lets them go home feeling contented and happy.

Tragedy provides no such relief. Yet we also say that we *enjoy* a good performance of *Macbeth*, *King Lear* or *Hamlet*. This is the crucial problem of much of the theoretical writing about tragedy. It is the problem of catharsis, the psychological effect of true tragedy. Usually it is said that we feel elated after a great tragedy because we have seen a superior human being facing adversity and misfortune nobly and with courage and dignity. So even if Lear and Hamlet have suffered and died, human nature in its nobility and grandeur has been triumphantly reaffirmed. There is certainly a great deal in this explanation. But does it always work? In a play like Georg Buchner's *Woyzeck*, one of the greatest plays of German dramatic literature, the central character is a mentally subnormal private soldier who kills his mistress because she has been unfaithful to him with a sergeant. He is distressed, hysterical, pitiful, yet, basically the play reaffirms the concept of human dignity which it shows to be present even in so lowly a person, or perhaps even more so in him than anyone else. The experience of sharing another human being's fate with deep compassion, of having gained a profound, lasting insight into human nature and man's predicament in this world produces an emotion akin to a religious feeling; and this feeling of having been touched by something beyond and outside our mundane everyday experience, having gained an insight into the workings of destiny, produces the sublime, cathartic effect of tragedy.

Comedy, on the other hand, remains on the everyday level. It gives us insights not into the ultimate crises of human life and the highest emotions associated with them, but insights, nevertheless, into the manners and ways of society, the little foibles and eccentricities of human behaviour. In *Tartuffe* it is bigotry and hypocrisy that are shown to us in action, in *The Importance of Being Earnest* (a very different kind of comedy) the snobbery of a certain kind of upper class behaviour, in Gogol's *The Government Inspector* the corruption of small town society in Tsarist Russia and much more besides.

Does farce give us insights? It is arguable. One might say farce exists merely to make us laugh. I personally feel that at its best, as in the farces of Feydeau or the cinematic

Tragedy, comedy, tragi-comedy

farces of Chaplin, Buster Keaton and Laurel and Hardy, farce too gives us insights—into the mechanics and automatisms of our frantic pursuits of sex or status, or the way in which society hammers the little man.

For centuries comedy and tragedy were strictly separated genres. It was axiomatic that you could not mix them. But there were always exceptions. In the First Folio of Shakespeare, *Troilus and Cressida* stands between the Comedies and the Tragedies: it is both comic and tragic—a tragi-comedy.

In the last seventy years tragi-comedy has come to the fore. The very fact that Chekhov's great plays can be seen both as tragedies and as comedies points to their actual nature as tragi-comedies. And the work of Brecht, Wedekind, Ionesco, Beckett and much of Pirandello belongs to the same mixed genre. For the director these plays are of particular difficulty: some must be played with complete seriousness and will then produce a comic effect; others must be played in a comic vein and produce deep sadness and tragic insight; others again demand a constant switching from one vein to the other, from scene to scene.

Tragi-comedy is thus a complex genre and one which demands a very high degree of sophistication from the audience. For the effect for the audience of all drama depends, ultimately, on a subtle interplay of expectations and their fulfilment. The style with which a play opens, as I pointed out earlier, prepares the way in which the audience tunes in its expectations: the costumes, the set, whether the language is prose or verse, whether the characters have red noses or noble, tragic features, determines whether the spectators will look forward to laughter or tears, gentle amusement or shattering emotions.

The modern, highly sophisticated, tragi-comic genre produces much of its effect by the sudden disappointment

75

and redirection of these expectations. An unsophisticated audience is bound to be thrown and disconcerted by it. It is not able to switch its mind quickly enough from one mode to another. For the more sophisticated spectator, on the other hand, these sudden shocks, these unexpected readjustments, are a source of pleasure and insight: tensions are created and relieved, riddles set which the spectator must solve. Brecht's *Verfremdungseffekt*, the strange-making effect which ultimately boils down to emotions being aroused and then suddenly and also sometimes brutally inhibited, is an essentially tragi-comic device; so also is Beckett's mixture of comedy, farce and despair in *Waiting for Godot*. The characters are dressed and behave like music-hall clowns, their patter is that of red-nosed comedians, yet the play depicts no less than the tragic position of man in an empty universe which may have a meaning, yet one which remains forever hidden from us. This is a case of playing farce and producing a tragic effect.

The theory of genres deals with abstract concepts of great importance and purity. Its study is essential for anyone who wants to understand drama and through it human nature itself.

In dealing with the theory of genres we must, however, never forget that in the concrete world the archetypes, the pure ideal concepts, always appear in an impure form. In theatrical practice the only real test is whether a play works or not as theatre. The theory of genres can be a very important aid to the director because it enables him to make essential decisions about the style in which a text is to be acted and produced. But, as Brecht was fond of saying, the proof of the pudding is always in the eating: which does not mean, however, that the rules of cookery are not also of the utmost importance.

8 The stage and the media

The basic unity of the dramatic mode of communication in the theatre and in the mass media of the cinema, television and radio seems to me a fact too obvious to argue about. After all, stage plays are filmed, televised, and broadcast on radio, suitably adapted, of course, but not modified in the essence of their mode of expression; conversely stage plays are made out of film scenarios (the successful stage musical *A Little Night Music* started life as an Ingmar Bergman film); television plays (like Pinter's *The Lover* and *The Collection*) are successfully produced in the theatre; television shows feature films daily and unsophisticated viewers can hardly tell the difference between these and series or plays specially made for television; and many plays which started as radio drama have ended up on the stage as well as the screen (notably Robert Bolt's *A Man for All Seasons*, originally written for radio and then televised, staged and filmed; or Bill Naughton's *Alfie*, also originally a radio script; even the longest run of all time, Agatha Christie's *The Mousetrap*, began as a radio play called *Three Blind Mice*).

An even more striking confirmation of the basic unity of the four different modes of dramatic presentation is the constant interchange of writers, directors, actors between them. The skills involved may be different in each case, but these differences are merely modifications of one basic dramatic craft.

It seems all the more strange to me, therefore, that the literature about the aesthetics and techniques of drama appears to be almost exclusively devoted to stage drama, while the voluminous and highly sophisticated literature about the cinema takes very little notice of the basic concepts of drama in a wider sense. (An honourable exception here is Jean-Luc Godard who freely acknowledges his indebtedness to Bertolt Brecht as a theorist of stage drama.

Yet it is, I believe, precisely from a recognition of the fundamental unity of drama as drama that a true appreciation of the differences between the distinct dramatic media must take its starting point. Moreover, it is from that vantage point to that the way in which the technical media themselves have in turn reinfluenced stage drama can be fully appreciated.

Being mechanically reproduceable and therefore (with very few exceptions in television and radio, where live presentation of drama once existed but has now practically died out) pre-recorded, the media have both gained and lost as against stage drama. Stage drama, being 'live', has the excitement of spontaneity, however well-rehearsed it may be, and it has—this is its main asset as against any mechanically reproduced drama—the feedback from the audience to the actors. On the other hand, mechanical pre-recording gives the director an infinitely greater scope for varying the venue of the action, much greater flexibility in structuring it through devices like montage and editing. The photographic nature of the film and television medium, moreover, allows a much

78

greater degree of realism in the backgrounds. On the other hand, this same photographic element also militates against anything stylised, removed from realism; even costume drama becomes a problem in the cinema and in television—the further the period of the action recedes from the present, the greater becomes the clash between the realism of the backgrounds and costumes and the contemporaneity of the language used by the characters. Verse drama becomes an even greater problem, which can be solved, but only with great ingenuity and only if the director is fully aware that he is battling against an inherent difficulty of his medium.

But the most essential difference between the stage and all three mechanical media lies elsewhere: the camera and the microphone are extensions of the director, his eye and ear; they enable him to choose his point of view (or hearing) and to move the audience there by varying long-shots and close-ups, by cutting from one face, one locale, to another at will. If a character is looking at another character's hand, the director can force the audience to look at it too, by cutting to it in close-up. In the mechanical media the director's power over the audience's point of view is total. On the stage, where the frame around the picture always remains the same, the single member of the audience is free to look at that hand, or to look elsewhere; in fact there each member of the audience selects his own camera angles and thus himself performs the work which the director takes on for him in cinema and television and (*mutatis mutandis*) in radio. This difference again gives the stage advantages and disadvantages. On the stage a director may fail to focus the audience's attention on the action he wants to emphasise; in the cinema this cannot happen. On the other hand the complex and subtle orchestration of a scene involving many characters (a feature of Chekhov on the stage) becomes very much more difficult in the cinema or in television. The sense of complexity, of more going on than one can take in with one glance, the richness of an intricate counterpoint of human contrasts, will inevitably be reduced in a medium which clearly leads the eye of the spectator rather than allows it to roam at will.

Another important aspect of the difference between the dramatic media concerns the psychology of the conditions under which the act of communication takes place. Here the cinema and the stage are on one side of the dividing line in that they are presented to crowds of people more or less fixed in their seats, an audience which has deliberately come to see something and will, in the great majority of cases, want to watch it to the end; on the other side of the dividing line are the electronic media which are received in the recipients' own homes and can be switched on and off at will and which, moreover, tend to be watched and listened to by very small groups of people or even isolated individuals. While the theatre or the cinema auditorium thus presents the conditions of mass psychology—the infectiousness of laughter, the mutual reinforcement of the audience reaction through the feed-back effect of observing (and imitating) one's neighbours—the electronic media have to count on individual reactions. Horror, for example (as in *Grand Guignol* theatre or the horror movie), produces quite a different effect in a crowd, which gives reassurance to each individual from that which ensues when a single, highly nervous spectator is exposed to it as a television viewer. For the isolated target of the electronic media the possibility of looking around him and seeing others not as frightened as he is will be missing and the final result, even if it does not lead to panic, will be far less pleasant than the delicious *frisson* which results from fear which, at the same time, is clearly understood to be only a harmless entertainment.

On the stage the distance between the spectator and the action is constant, in the media it varies: with a close-up or, a whispered internal monologue on radio, the audience is experiencing the utmost proximity and intimacy with the action; in long-shots it is moved to a great distance. In television, where, at least under present technological conditions, the screen is still relatively small and the detail in long-distance shots therefore much reduced, the most effective shots are close-ups or medium-distance shots. Hence the strength of television drama tends to lie in the intimacy with which it can bring a relatively small number of characters into contact with the viewer; most of the best dramatic writing for television has profited from this closeness and intimacy. Samuel Beckett's television play *Eh Joe!* is a case in point: here only one person is seen; the camera relentlessly comes nearer to him step by step, while we—and he—hear the voice of a woman whose unhappiness he has caused. In the end the camera has come so near to the man's face that nothing remains but the blackness of the horror-stricken wide-open pupils of his eyes. Here Beckett uses the internal monologue in close conjunction with the terrifying intimacy of the television camera.

The internal monologue is usually regarded as the domain of drama on radio. The absence of the visual dimension forces the radio listener to visualise the action of the play for himself, placing it literally inside his own head, his own imagination, and thus makes the world of fantasy, dream, memory and man's inner life the ideal subject-matter for radio drama. The objective world can be conjured up—and much radio drama is as realistic as the cinema—but the fact that even this objective picture of the real world is internalised by the listener presents the radio dramatist with the opportunity of sliding from the real into an imaginary world, often leaving it to the audience to decide whether they have experienced reality or fantasy, dream or fact. The counterpoint between people's overt conversation and the private thoughts which accompany it (which Eugene O'Neill tried to achieve by rather laborious means in stage play like *Strange Interlude*) is a commonplace of radio drama, easily achieved by its techniques.

One of the essential differences between the instant electronic mass media and both the theatre and the cinema is their continuousness; to see a play in the theatre or even in the cinema is still an occasion, with its sense of being so whereas drama on television and on radio forms part of a continuous stream of news, information and entertainment. The need to structure such a continuous stream is as important as the need to structure the flow of events within a given dramatic work; it produces a veritable craving, both on the part of the programme makers and on the part of the recipients, for fixed points, regularly recurring features at set and easily recognisable times (news on the hour, a favourite serial every Tuesday at 7·30 pm, etc). This is why drama on television and radio has a strong tendency towards being grouped in series. Familiar fictional characters (the detective, the policeman, the doctor) or whole families or groups of characters who return regularly at fixed times every week (every day in the case of 'soap opera') are perhaps the most characteristic contribution of the electronic media to drama. The series form in many ways makes the craft of the writer easier for once he is into a series there is no need for him to spend time or ingenuity on an exposition introducing his chief characters at the beginning of each episode; they are already well known to the audience. This makes the dramatic series fairly economical in its use of time: the story can start *in medias res.*

The main characters of such series, which may go on for many years, acquire a very peculiar reality for the audience; they become so familiar, the fusion between the character and the actor so complete, that they tend to become akin to mythological heroes, which means that they may be taken to be more real than real public figures. Thus the weddings or deaths of purely fictional personalities often acquire the importance of public events, comparable to one involving a real statesman or hero of sport.

The emergence of these new heroes of folk myth from drama on the mass media underlines the new importance of dramatic forms of expression in our time.

The very fact that playwrights like Brecht (who wrote for radio, the stage and the cinema), Beckett (who has written stage plays, radio plays, and a television play as well as a film), Pinter (who straddles all four dramatic media), Osborne, Wesker, Robert Bolt have worked in all or most of the different dramatic media, and freely and easily move between them, reinforces my initial contention that despite their technological and aesthetic differences, all of them are ultimately one as drama. The brief history of the new media has already produced an extremely stimulating cross-fertilisation, from which the live theatre was by no means the last to profit. The breakdown of the rigid structure of the well-made play, the ease with which cinematic techniques are now accepted by the audiences of live theatre (very brief scenes cross-cutting each other) and indeed the easy acceptance of narration (which returned to the theatre via radio) are all very clear indications of the influence of the new media upon the old.

There can be no doubt that this intermingling of the dramatic media will continue in the future, and increasingly so. The live theatre, particularly its ability to produce experiments with a minimum of technical means and cost, must continue to be of immense importance for the more cumbersome technological media with their vast requirement of expensive equipment, as a training ground for new ideas and new talent and a proving ground for new ideas which would, untried, not justify a large investment of capital or resources. Conversely the mass media are opening up a huge new audience for the dramatic form of communication. People who would never have gone to the theatre throughout their lives are now exposed to vast quantities of dramatic material on television and radio (at least in Europe where radio drama is still a strong ingredient of public service broadcasting) and this in turn will inevitably produce a large new and sophisticated audience clamouring for work of high literary and artistic value and intellectual level which only a minority medium such as the live theatre can ultimately provide. The expansion of repertory and regional theatre in Britain and the United States, countries which until comparatively recent times lacked a non-commercial sector in the theatre, already testifies to the effects of the spread of dramatic modes of communication via the mass media. And it is not only audiences which are created by the spread of drama on the media, but also creative talent fostered. Many of the younger generation of British playwrights had their initial interest in dramatic forms of expression awakened by radio and television drama. Many of them came from areas and social backgrounds which, in an earlier epoch, would never have brought them into contact with theatre and thus their talent might never have been discovered and stimulated at all.

Throughout the history of drama its development has been a process of differentiation: opera, ballet, the mime play, the puppet play, the music hall, the circus—all these are ultimately dramatic forms which have attained semi-autonomous status. The coming of drama in cinema, television and radio has continued this process of differentiation, but, curiously enough, here the relationship with traditional drama is stronger than that, say, between opera and straight drama. And just as the mutual cross-fertilisation of all branches of drama is a continuous process, the live theatre taking ideas from ballet or opera and vice versa, so it will continue with even greater intensity between the stage and the technical media. And in the ideas about mixed-media shows, happenings and other forms of new dramatic or theatrical experiences we have portents for the future which show that this process of differentiation and cross-fertilisation is bound to go on.

9 *Illusion and reality*

Drama—theatre—is mimetic action, an imitation of the real world as play, as make-believe. The drama we see in the theatre and for that matter on the television screen or in the cinema is an elaborately manufactured illusion. And yet, compared to other illusion-producing arts, drama—a dramatic text in performance—contains a far greater element of reality.

Take a painting. It produces an illusion of a landscape, a house, the likeness of a human being in a portrait—and the only real elements it contains are paints and canvas. A play also produces an illusion, say, of Hamlet in the castle at Elsinore. But here Hamlet, the young man on the stage—long dead as a historical figure, perhaps never having lived and so a pure figment of the playwright's imagination—is portrayed by a young man, an actor who really is a young man. And he is sitting on a chair which really is a chair. That that chair is supposed to be in a Danish castle centuries ago is the illusion we are asked to accept, but the chair is a chair nevertheless. Drama in performance, therefore, in contrast to all other illusion-producing arts, contains, it might be said, a higher proportion of reality. Indeed, there have been performances of *Hamlet* in the real castle of Elsinore, so the chair Hamlet was sitting on really was a chair in real Elsinore. And if we extend the range of drama outside the theatre to television or the cinema: whole sequences of dramatic action can be acted out and recorded as happening in the real location of the play, whether that is an episode of *Z Cars* filmed in the streets of a real Northern town in real police cars, *The Merchant of Venice* filmed in Venice, or *Romeo and Juliet* in Verona.

This seems to me one of the chief characteristics of drama and one of its chief fascinations: that a play in performance is a fusion of the wholly imaginary—the products of a writer's imagination fixed once and for all and, in that sense, a dead letter—with an element of the living reality of the actors, their costumes, the furniture which surrounds them, the things they handle, such as swords or fans or knives and forks. Every performance of a play from past centuries can thus be seen as an act of resurrection: the dead words and actions are reincarnated by the living presence of the actors. No wonder that theatrical jargon talks of a performance of an old play as a revival.

In the purely academic study of drama, attention tends quite naturally to focus on the element most readily available for study: the text, the play as literature. The quality of the other elements, the performance, the lighting, the magnetism of the actors, is far more elusive and was, before the invention of mechanical recording techniques, almost totally lost. Yet these are the elements which play the decisive part in attracting audiences to the theatre (or to the cinema, or to television viewing) and which, if we really analysed the impact of a theatrical experience on audiences, would also, I am sure, be found to account for the bulk of the enjoyment the audience derives from a theatrical experience.

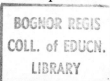

In the live theatre it is this aspect of the fusion of a fixed element (the text) with a fluid element (the actors) which makes every single performance a wholly distinct work of art—even within a long run of one play with the same cast, sets, lighting, etc. In the classical Chinese theatre where the standard texts are all well-known to the audiences, and are also extremely long, only extracts from the complete texts are performed because the audiences, who take the texts for granted, mainly come to see how certain actors will perform them.

Very similarly, our own classical drama, above all Shakespeare, becomes the basis of our judgement on actors: we go to *Hamlet* or for the nth time because we are interested to see how Scofield's Hamlet differs from Gielgud's, Burton's, O'Toole's, etc. (In the last decade the function of the director as a factor in the variable portion of the theatrical experience has added an element to the attractions of going to see a well-known standard text, we now also go to see Peter Hall's, Peter Brook's, Giorgio Strehler's, Roger Planchon's *Hamlet*, *King Lear* or *Macbeth*.)

Not everything in the theatre, therefore, is illusion. We are not really seeing Macbeth fighting a battle outside his castle at Dunsinane, but we have come to see Sir John Gielgud or Richard Burton and we see that actor, the real man, hear his voice, which gives us particular pleasure. Moreover, when we see him fight with Macduff we admire the two actors' skill; we know that Macbeth is not really being killed, but we see two human beings really fencing. When the renown of English actors in Shakespeare's time had spread throughout Europe, English companies of strolling players toured European countries, notably Germany. The audiences did not understand the text but they marvelled at the skill with which these actors fought and danced, they paid their entrance money mainly to see their acrobatic feats and the grace of their movements when dancing. The most popular play was Marlowe's *Jew of Malta* where the chief villain falls into a cauldron of boiling oil with the utmost acrobatic dexterity.

In these aspects the theatre comes very close to another area where man's play instinct is manifested—sport. Theatre can be seen as a spectator sport. And if you watch a very great actor like Laurence Olivier you will notice that his evident enjoyment of the physical aspects of acting (as when he balances on the edge of a chair, fixing a light bulb in O'Neill's *Long Day's Journey into Night* or tumbles down a long flight of steps as the dying Coriolanus, not to mention the vast voice range in his Othello) forms a decisive element in his impact as well as in his approach to the art of acting.

The actor is and will always remain the keystone of all drama. Ballet which has no text at all (and in which sheer physical prowess, athleticism, is at the very core of the performance); the mime play of great artists like Debureau or our contemporary Marcel Marceau, which also has no spoken text at all; or the improvised Commedia dell'arte of the Italian Renaissance which had a text, but one which was not written down and prerehearsed, and which spontaneously arose in performance; or the masterpieces in the silent cinema—all these are types of drama with a minimal content of literature. There can thus be drama without a text.

It is in the actor that the elements of reality and illusion meet: have we come to see Othello as played by Olivier, or Olivier playing Othello? There is a creative tension between the fictitious character imagined by the playwright and the real man who lends that figment of a poet's fancy his solid physical reality, plus—and this is very important—additional imagination, additional poetic invention of gesture, action, intonation, timing. It has been said, and rightly, that there is poetry in the theatre as well as a peculiar poetry of the theatre. Poetry in the theatre is the poetic language created by the playwright; but much of the poetry of the theatre arises from a look, an entrance, a pause. And these are the creations, in most cases, of actors and directors.

Certainly in the commercial theatre it is the star who is the decisive factor in raising the capital for a production. Playwrights offer their manuscripts to leading actors in the hope that their desire to appear in the play will enable it to be performed.

Many of the most successful actors reduce the element of fiction in their appearances to a minimum. These actors are essentially exhibitors of themselves; far from trying to create the illusion of being the character the playwright imagined, they lend that imagined character the reality of their attraction.

You can see this best exemplified perhaps in English Christmas pantomime where the fairytale framework of Dick Whittington or Cinderella serves merely as the flimsiest of pretexts for a series of star turns and where the principal boy, say Prince Charming in *Cinderella*, quite clearly is less intent on portraying a fairytale prince than displaying her splendid legs in tights. Far from looking down on this as a degradation of the theatrical art, I consider it a triumphant affirmation of one of the most enduring strengths of theatre.

For although the theatre is a house of illusion, the illusion is never complete. Think of the eighteenth-century peasant who responded to Richard III's cry 'My kingdom for a horse' with the offer of his own nag. The great actor playing Richard replied: 'Come up yourself, an ass will do!' This old anecdote shows a spectator not sophisticated enough to appreciate the delicate balance between illusion and reality on which the magic of the theatre depends. We who are more skilled in appreciating drama are, in fact, getting our pleasure at two levels at the same time: in watching *Othello* we are deeply moved by the misfortunes of the hero, but at the very same moment when tears come into our eyes at his downfall, we also, almost schizophrenically, say to ourselves: 'How brilliantly Olivier held that pause! How beautifully he achieved that effect by a mere raising of an eyebrow.'

In modern drama, playwrights have become more conscious than ever of the potential of that tension between illusion and reality, fact and fiction, in the theatrical experience. Pirandello used it in *Six Characters in Search of an Author* by going so far as to show us the actors as they really are as private individuals assembled for a rehearsal, then the characters as imagined by the author, and then these characters as portrayed by those actors. Brecht insisted that the audience should be actively encouraged not to be taken in by any pretence that what they are seeing on the stage is more than mere fiction. In his own production of Sophocles' *Antigone* in the little town of Chur in Switzerland in 1948, Brecht actually had the actors on stage while they were not acting. They sat around the acting area, which was delineated by four poles at its four corners, and Brecht suggested they might be seen reading the evening paper, eating a sandwich or adjusting their costume. As their cue approached they were seen to get up, making last-minute preparations for their entrance, and as they crossed the boundary of the acting area the audience could actually

91

experience the moment at which they assumed the stance and movement of the character.

Here the contrast between the real little Miss Smith who lives in Chiswick and whose boyfriend is a student at the Royal College of Art and the Greek Princess Antigone who is prepared to die for the honour of her dead brother is being turned into a powerful artistic device. Not only would the audience be able to appreciate the skill by which the actress, the real Miss Smith, turns herself into the tragic heroine; in Brecht's view it would also enable them to appreciate both what the Greek heroine has in common with a modern girl and what separates them.

Similarly, in the work of playwrights like Beckett and Ionesco, the audience is never left in any doubt that what they are seeing is not meant to produce an illusion of reality, that they are merely watching people who are trying to show them something by playful pretence. In *Waiting for Godot* the characters more than once refer to the presence of the audience. Ionesco, in the first version of his *Bald Primadonna*, wanted to finish the play with the author coming on stage and insulting the audience. He was dissuaded from doing this, but now the play ends by starting again at the point where it began—a device which clearly indicates the artificiality of the occasion. Over a hundred years ago, in the Epilogue to *The Inspector General*, Gogol deliberately destroyed the illusion by hurling at the audience, 'What are you laughing at? It's yourselves you are laughing at!'

The latest wave of the theatrical avant-garde goes even further in exploiting these tensions between the real and the imaginary. The American avant-garde troupe *The Living Theatre*, which toured Europe for several years, developed a technique which made reality and illusion merge in new ways. The actors involved the audience in discussions, which were real enough; fights developed between members of the audience and some of the actors. These fights were real, in the sense that people pushed each other, hurled insults and occasionally came to blows; yet when I asked Julian Beck, one of the leaders of the company, whether the situation had really got out of hand at a performance I had attended the night before, he replied that the incident was intentional and occurred every night, simply because the actors had mastered the complex psychological technique of both provoking such fights and then stopping them again at will by letting something happen elsewhere in the auditorium which drew away the attention of all concerned. Here theatre veers away from fiction and becomes a manipulation of reality. Is it then theatre still? That is a moot point of definition. It is certainly a borderline case. But the borderlines of definitions of a phenomenon like the theatre are always bound to be extremely fluid.

This type of modern avant-garde theatre gives rise to a number of very deep questions. The member of the audience who feels insulted and starts to kick the actor who has insulted him is really angry, the actor has really insulted him, and yet both are part of a spectacle produced for the delight, or the emotional disturbance, of an audience and in that sense they are theatre. But, the authors of such a spectacle may argue, a good deal of our ordinary life outside the theatre is similarly artificial. The traffic warden who fines the illegally parked motorist may say 'I'm sorry for you, I don't want to hurt you but in my capacity as traffic warden I have to fine you.' Once he has donned the uniform of a traffic warden, the real personal emotions of the individual concerned must be suppressed and he must play the role society has cast him in, including the wearing of the appropriate costume, the speaking of the appropriate jargon, and the performance of actions which he would not want to perform in his private capacity.

There is thus much theatre, much role-playing, much illusion in ordinary life. Shakespeare spoke of the world being a stage and all men and women merely players, actors on it. And of course the nature of reality itself is problematic. Our senses are fallible; we can perceive reality only through these imperfect senses and so what we perceive may itself be an illusion. Indeed, judged with the knowledge of a physicist, our perception of everyday reality is illusion.

So in effect the theatre, which merely adds another dimension of illusion to the fabric of illusion we call reality, is a perfect image of our situation as human beings in this world. To quote Shakespeare

> ...These our actors,
> As I foretold you, were all spirits, and
> Are melted into air, into thin air,
> And like the baseless fabric of this vision,
> The cloud-capped towers, the gorgeous palaces,
> The solemn temples, the great globe itself,
> Yea, all which it inherit, shall dissolve
> And like this insubstantial pageant faded
> Leave not a rack behind. We are such stuff
> As dreams are made on; and our little life
> Is rounded with a sleep.

10   Drama and society

A great deal has been spoken and written in the last decades about politically committed art, and especially about political theatre, drama as an instrument of social and political change. And there can be no doubt that the theatre—and drama in its wider connotation which extends to the cinema and the electronic mass media—is a powerful political weapon. The use made of the theatre in totalitarian societies of all types is a widely noticed and discussed phenomenon of our times, and indeed, in the past, the reluctance of British governments over a very long period to subsidise something like a National Theatre was frequently buttressed with the argument that if the government of the day was the paymaster, the danger existed that drama would be censored, influenced, or used as an instrument for the propagation of the ruling party's political line. The creation of a body like the Arts Council of Great Britain, which acts as a buffer between the government and the theatres served the purpose of neutralising just such a danger.

Yet I am convinced that the power of drama to act as a tool of direct political propaganda is over-estimated. One could formulate this in another way by stating that those who call for politically committed drama in support of their own cause overestimate the short-term propaganda effect of theatre.

Why? Because of the peculiar nature of drama as an instrument of knowledge, of perception, thought, insight about society, its concreteness and the fact that drama never makes an overt statement, that by its very nature it is always an experiment which always carries its own control-mechanism, its own verification, within it.

Let me explain what I mean by outlining a possible case. During the debate on some basic issue like the campaign for the abolition of the death penalty a playwright wants to write a powerful piece against hanging. So he may invent a story about a murder, in which the victim is as guilty as the murderer: let us assume that a person who has been blackmailed has killed his tormentor in a fit of passion. The playwright will then show the agony of the condemned man during and after his trial, etc. He will be tempted, in order to achieve his very laudable aim, to weight the case as much against the death penalty, as much in favour of the condemned man as possible. If he does that, the supporters of the death penalty will come out as black villains, determined on punishment as revenge. But, if the author concerned yields to this temptation, the effect of the play will nevertheless be quite different from the one he intended. For his exaggeratedly villainous characters will appear as cardboard figures and in performance the audience will remain uncovinced of the truth of the argument.

Of course, if the playwright concerned is a really good dramatist he will not yield to that temptation; he will be quite unable to yield to it, simply because a good dramatist, in writing his play, must experience all the feelings of each one of his characters from the inside, however much he may disapprove of them—witness Shakespeare's

96

Richard III. So he will be bound to show that the judge who pronounces the sentence also suffers agonies in his mind, he will have to show the case for the punishment of his victim as much and as fairly as that against it. Perhaps he will have to let us see the sufferings of the family of the murder victim, the consequences of letting a murder go unpunished on other potential murderers, and so on. If he is a good dramatist he will still make his case against the death penalty. But he will not be able to stop at least some members of his audience from seeing the other side of the case as well. Ultimately the effect will depend not so much on the manifest intention of the author as on the quality of the play as drama. If the play is accepted by the consensus of the audience as a convincing picture of the situation, which will always have two sides from which it can be seen, it will have a profound effect, but a long-term one, by lingering in the minds of the audience and by gradually making them realise the complexity of the situation depicted. And that long-term effect may be quite different from the one immediately intended.

There can be little doubt, for instance, that Shake-speare in writing *The Merchant of Venice* intended the character of Shylock to be that of a hateful and detestable usurer. But, because Shakespeare was the great dramatist he was he did feel himself into the mind of the greedy Jew and his motivations: so he made Shylock suffer from the hatred and the injustice with which Jews were treated and gave him some magnificent speeches to make us aware of these motivations. As a result, a modern performance frequently arouses as much sympathy for Shylock as detestation of his greed. What may have started as anti-Semitic propaganda turns out to be a source of sympathy for a racial minority. Or take another play by Shake-speare: *Twelfth Night*. The character of Malvolio is clearly designed as an attack on the narrow-minded, hypocritical Puritan. Yet when it comes to it, the sufferings of that character, about whose discomfiture we are clearly supposed to be happy, are most graphically, convincingly and movingly experienced by Malvolio himself (and clearly also in the playwright's imagination). As a result, in many performances of the play I have felt deeply sorry for and greatly in sympathy with that poor, frustrated victim of a practical joke played on him by arrogant people who thought that because they were socially superior they could subject a lower-class person to any indignity they wanted, merely to have a good laugh.

The more completely a playwright imagines a situation and the characters in it, the nearer the play will come to the complexity and ambivalence of the real world. This is not to say that a play, whether overtly political or not, will not have a political effect. Indeed, playwrights like Ibsen or Shaw have contributed greatly to important social and therefore ultimately political changes. Ibsen was a very important influence in opening up the discussion of the position of women in society and did, in fact, I believe, make a decisive contribution to the change which started with women's suffrage and which is still going on today under the heading of the women's liberation movement. Nora in *A Doll's House* started a discussion about the position of women in Victorian marriage; Mrs Alving in *Ghosts* drew attention to the double standards of morality for men and women; and *Hedda Gabler* ultimately constitutes a plea to allow women to develop their creativeness. Shaw's brilliant and amusing demonstration of his socialist point of view contributed much to the rise of left-wing thinking in Britian and elsewhere, whether he dealt with social topics such as slums in *Widower's Houses* or prostitution in *Mrs Warren's Profession* or with general political ideas, as in *Man and Superman*. Yet, if we look at Ibsen's plays as well as Shaw's, it is remarkable how fairly—in spite of their political purpose—they stated the problem: how often, in Shaw's *Major Barbara*, the case for big business was as powerfully and sympathetically stated as the one against big business; or, indeed, in his *St Joan*, how intelligently the prosecution's case is argued against Joan at her trial.

Bertolt Brecht, one of the most deeply and passionately committed playwrights of our time, always refused to make his message too explicit because he knew, instinctively as well as consciously, that what matters is the posing of the problem in a way which will compel the audience to think for themselves, rather than drumming some message into their heads. In his *Galileo* the Roman Catholic Church's case for stopping free scientific inquiry (a case which Brecht wholly rejected and abominated) is stated with the utmost power, intelligence and persuasiveness, simply because otherwise the case for free scientific inquiry would have been weakened by being made to appear less intelligent, less convincing than it really is. While rehearsing the play in East Germany shortly before he died, Brecht argued so passionately for getting his actors to put the Church's standpoint with such total conviction that he suddenly stopped himself and smilingly remarked: 'I seem to be the only person in this country still arguing for the Pope.'

In the case of *Mother Courage* Brecht was actually reproached by communist party spokesmen for refusing to hammer the pacifist, anti-militarist point of the play home to the audience by making his anti-heroine, the war-profiteer trader, realise the error of her ways. He refused to add a political exhortation or an unconvincing change of heart to the play. And yet we know from his own writings that he was worried by the fact that his anti-heroine tended, even in his own production, to be pitied and admired by the spectators as a heroic figure rather than regarded as a cautionary example.

It is very revealing to see how over-propagandist drama defeats its own ends. For, unlike printed literature, which is consumed by individuals alone, the theatre is a collective experience. The reaction it evokes happens in public. Thus the message (political or otherwise) which a play contains always coexists with a demonstration of its reception by a social unit, the collectivity of the audience. In Nazi Germany certain plays which were acknowledged German classics and were regarded by the Nazis themselves as important elements in the cultural heritage of the nation, nevertheless had to be banned because audiences tended to applaud too loudly: for example, in Schiller's *Don Carlos* in which a powerful plea for freedom of speech is made. Similarly, totalitarian regimes can ill afford to have passages praising the leader and his works received by their audiences in sullen silence. They can tolerate even less having the theatres showing such plays standing empty. At the height of Stalinism the Soviet theatres were in that danger. Not, I think, because the population was hostile, but because the political message of most plays was so overdone, and so predictable, that everyone knew what it would be even before the curtain went up, and such plays therefore became terribly dull. The 'thaw' of 1965 in Poland and Hungary, and that of 1966 and 1967 in Czechoslovakia, was preceded by crises in the theatre. In order to fill the gapingly empty auditoria the authorities had to allow more popular plays, and these had to include classics

Drama and society

dispensing a nationalistic or traditionalist message, as well as contemporary plays which dealt with topical themes by sly allusion or allegory and were instantly understood by audiences as containing a message of criticism of existing conditions. Although the electronic mass media and the cinema do not confront a collective audience and the actors in the same direct fashion, in the long term the social impact of drama in these media is similar: only here the reaction takes time to form. The rigid control of the cinema in totalitarian societies like Nazi Germany and the Soviet Union, and the even more restrictive use of drama in television and radio in such societies, amply demonstrates the concern of those regimes about the impact of drama.

Even in countries with greater overt freedom the theatre inevitably plays an important part in bringing into the open what are the burning issues of the time, such as capital punishment, social legislation and indeed the debate for and against socialism. In France, in the United States and in Britain the theatrical avant-garde has always been the spearhead of new trends of social and political thought. The theatre is the place where a nation thinks in public in front of itself. And in that context all sorts of matters assume political importance, for, ultimately, there is a close link between the general beliefs of a society, its concept of proper behaviour and good manners, its view of sexual morals, and the political climate of a nation. Changes in manners and mores may ultimately change the very temper of politics.

An example which is often quoted in this context is that of Shaw's *Pygmalion*. During its first performance in 1913 that fearful taboo word in English Victorian society, 'bloody', was for the first time pronounced upon the stage in front of a respectable audience. Basil Dean, the veteran

101

producer, who was Beerbohm Tree's assistant at this occasion, has told me how everyone in the audience as well as behind the scenes dreaded the moment, which rumour had anticipated, when all the hitherto valid codes of polite behaviour would be broken. And when Eliza Doolittle had actually uttered the awful phrase 'not bloody likely', Dean tells me one could feel a sigh of relief rising from the auditorium of His Majesty's Theatre. The taboo had been broken, the heavens had not fallen, but something epoch-making had happened. Whether one welcomed the development or deplored it, from that moment the fabric of Victorian upper-class manners had begun to crumble. All that had happened was that a funny line had passed the lips of a favourite actress, Mrs Patrick Campbell. On the surface, a less political event could hardly have been imagined. And yet, however long-term, however indirectly, it was certainly symptomatic of a big change in society.

It is clearly very difficult to measure the impact of such symptomatic events accurately. Is the fact that it has become possible to speak certain words in public merely an indication of a change which has already happened, or does it actually initiate the change? My guess is that there is a more complex link between these two alternatives. The change has happened in the minds of a few people, an elite, an avant-garde. But the fact that it is brought into the open and seen to be accepted without overt indignation or sanctions against those who have dared to breach the taboo then becomes a further powerful factor in dissolving the taboo in the minds of those who were still afraid to breach it. In the last half-century the theatre's part in destroying the taboos surrounding the frank discussion of sexual matters, homosexuality, the use of strong language regarded as blasphemous, etc., has been spectacular in the English-speaking world. The success—and the acceptance—of plays like *The Boys in the Band* was clearly both a symptom of change and an agent of further changes in attitudes. And social attitudes of this kind are also important political facts.

Northrop Frye has observed that in drama we invariably see at the beginning what amounts to a social order which is being disturbed and is, in one way or another, either overthrown or re-established, albeit in a different form. In *Macbeth* this is only too obvious. One king is murdered; another king takes his place and is in turn removed. Yet take a play of a quite different nature, *The Winter's Tale*. There a king's family—and thus a country—is disrupted and at the end order is restored under the auspices of the next generation. And even in the conventional French amorous triangle, a marriage is threatened by the appearance of the wife's lover and in the end either the marriage is vindicated and the lover expelled, or a new set-up is introduced, the old order overthrown. There are always social implications in any dramatic situation and in the resolution of any dramatic conflict simply because all human situations, all human behaviour patterns, have social—and therefore also political—implications.

Hamlet speaks of the theatre holding a mirror up to nature. I think in fact it is society to which the theatre holds up the mirror. The theatre and all drama can be seen as a mirror in which society looks at itself. This also is a fact which has social and political implications: for example, that at certain times the theatre tended to show only middle-class people to middle-class people demonstrates that in those times the lower classes were effectively excluded from society and therefore from the theatre.

The manners and life-style shown in the theatre inevitably become a potent influence on the manners and life-style of the times. Unconsciously we tend to reflect in our own life the attitudes, the accepted modes of behaviour, we have seen in the theatre, or for that matter in the cinema or on television. How do courting couples know what to say to each other when for the first time they are in a situation where they have to find the right words to break the ice or to declare their feelings? I am certain that unconsciously they will use dialogue or a style of approach they have seen on the stage or screen. And similarly with people who are faced with death, bereavement, victory or defeat in sport, etc. Of course, the playwrights who wrote the dialogues concerned have imitated dialogues they have observed in real life. Yet they have selected the manner of speech and the words which they felt most appropriate, so they have reinforced a certain way of behaviour as against another. When Shaw made Eliza Doolittle say 'not bloody likely' he was, of course, copying a phrase that was widely in use. But when it could be spoken in a theatre, society in a way was allowing itself to use it more openly. (Whether this was a good thing or not is quite a different matter.) As playwrights on the whole tend to be members of the more adventurous and advanced section of society, the theatre will inevitably be an instrument of social innovation and in that sense it is an institution subversive of the *status quo*.

Much of what I have said here about drama could also be applied in some degree to other arts as well—for example, painting, or indeed the novel. What distinguishes drama is that on the whole it is more accessible because it requires less concentration and also that its impact is far more immediate, direct and therefore powerful. In our own civilisation drama, in its mass-

Drama and society

produced and mass-consumed forms, will inevitably have a larger and more powerful impact than ever before in history. It is impossible to foresee the long-term effects of this immense expansion of drama as a vehicle of expression and communication, but there can be no doubt whatever that ultimately, inevitably it will contribute to great social changes.

11   The truth of drama

Most drama is fiction put before us in performance by real human beings; unlike purely literary fiction, it is thus made visible and palpable, given, as it were, the power and impact of the living flesh. These elements constitute a strong dose of reality in the fiction, they lend their reality to their authors' fantasy.

For all fiction, even the most naturalistic, the most strictly documentary play, can be seen as, and essentially is, a fantasy, a daydream of its author. The author of the most strictly researched and documented historical play is imagining the detail, the emotional tensions, the feelings of the characters, and then shaping his fantasies into an artistic form. If he shows Napoleon on the battlefield at Waterloo, he has to imagine what Napoleon felt there before writing down what he imagines him to have said or done.

It is a cliché of received folk wisdom that fiction is a form of lying. Being freed from the consequences which follow upon anything we say and do in the real world, the inventor of stories, of made-up situations, is free to indulge his most outrageous fancies. In that sense, stories and plays are lies. Yet, in another sense, they are important truths. They tell us something about the fantasies of

106

their authors, their daydreams and the visions which come to them when they give their imagination free rein. And such daydreams and imaginings and fantasies are truths which contain precious material about their creators' inner life and give us profound insights into the personality and psychology of the human beings who produce them.

Every piece of fiction, therefore, growing as it does out of its author's subconscious and conscious mind, is valuable as a human document. The drawings and writings of mental patients can be as valuable for a diagnosis and cure of their condition as are the dreams which patients relate to their psychoanalysts. Works of the art of fiction are clearly very different from the fantasies of such patients, but they also have certain features in common with them. The playwright writing dialogue for the character of Napoleon has to imagine himself into Napoleon's mind; the mental patient who is convinced that he is Napoleon does the same thing, but more intensely and without the ability to control his fantasy, to separate fiction from fact. But the main difference between the fantasies of mental patients and the art of fiction lies in the degree of relevance to large numbers of people, in the universality of art and, above all, in the degree of skill with which it shapes daydreams and fantasies. If it is the case that individuals indulge in daydreams and fantasy lives to relieve their individual psychological tensions, then the creations of artists have the power to relieve the psychological tensions of large numbers of individuals–as well as those of their authors. That is why reading fiction and watching drama are not only pleasurable activities but for many people a real *need*.

A playwright, in imagining his characters and the

dialogue they speak, must, if he is really skilful, enter into the feelings, the reactions, the personal manner of speech of each character. On the other hand, each character which thus emerges from the mind of its creator, will in some sense correspond to and represent certain aspects and elements in that playwright's personal experience and psychological make-up; imagination must always be based on at least a germ of personal experience. Thus we might say that in creating Macbeth Shakespeare had to draw upon that part of his own psychology which was ambitious and aggressive; yet in imagining Lady Macduff, who is so horribly murdered in the same play, Shakespeare had to draw on that part of himself which was gentle, loving and terrified of violence. Playwrights frequently speak of the phenomenon that characters, once imagined, acquire a certain autonomy of action, indeed, refuse to do what the playwright had originally planned. Put in different terms, this would mean that some of the elements in the playwright's personality, say the aggressive element in his make-up which infuses his characterisation of a murderer, have entered into conflict with other elements in his make-up represented by other characters, just, as, once someone has started hitting his opponent in a fight, he might suddenly find himself unable to stop, although his law-abiding instincts strongly urge him to do so. Pirandello's play *Six Characters in Search of an Author* directly deals with this side of a playwright's experience of his own art. Once having been imagined, and then discarded, these characters had acquired such a force of autonomy that they insist on coming to life on the stage. Why had Pirandello not wanted to go on with the discarded story? Did these characters suddenly confront him with a side of himself which he wanted to repress? Probably: and this is the subconscious conflict within himself which he has dramatised with all the conscious skill and intelligence at his command.

These considerations are not merely interesting from the point of view of the psychology of the creative act of the playwright. They also have a very important bearing on the nature of drama itself. For they show that all fiction, drama included, is true, if not in the facts about the external circumstances outlined in the story and the characters, all the more so in the insights through the characters into the author's mind and through that into the way we all think and feel.

Eugène Ionesco has movingly described how, when he had written his first play, *The Bald Primadonna*, he regarded it as an outgrowth of his private obsessions, his private world which he considered utterly mad. He had no thought that it might appeal to anyone but himself and his family, who knew his private quirks. When the play, very much against his will, was put on the stage, it was, he says, a revelation to him to watch the audience's reaction: suddenly he realised that his own private idiosyncrasy, his secret craziness had something in common with everybody else's private craziness, and that feelings and fantasies he had thought were his own peculiar eccentricity, which made him different from all other people, could be understood and were shared by large numbers of human beings. This, he says, came as an immense relief to him–and no doubt the laughter which greets plays like Ionesco's is a collective acknowledgement and expression of that same relief which comes as an instant release to all the members of the audience who realise that others react in the same way as themselves.

The complexity of drama and its ability to deal with the

whole gamut of human experience stem, I feel, from this aspect of its nature.

Literature which is designed for reading alone is far more straightforward, far more lineal or unidimensional than drama with its multiple levels of both expression and meaning, with its objectivity which puts the onus of interpretation on the recipient of the experience, the spectator. In this drama is like life itself. In all other forms of literary communication, in the very act of perceiving it–by reading a novel, listening to a poem–we are aware that we are apprehending words which have passed through the consciousness of another human being, the author of the novel or poem. If we are told something, we know that we are told it in the way the author wanted to tell it. And most such communication (the narrative in the novel, the description of emotion in the poem) is a package which includes the author's comment. Even the most'objective'type of novel, like the French *nouveau roman*, which concentrates on the most meticulously factual descriptions, never conceals, or wants to conceal, that these descriptions refer to the world as perceived by one subjective observer. The very act of telling a story in the novel or of evoking an emotion in lyrical poetry must be subjective and is necessarily perceived as such by the reader or listener.

In drama, on the other hand, however subjective the author's vision might have been when he wrote the play, the mode of presentation, the fact that it seems to be happening before our eyes as a simulated segment of concrete events embodied by human beings, makes us see the action as though it were an objective presence, something that occurs spontaneously before us and that we have to observe to evaluate it, form an opinion as to what it is and what it means. The audience in drama,

110

whether they want it or not, are compelled to arrive at their own interpretation (which might be quite different from the author's). If a character in a play makes a statement, we, the audience, have to make up our minds whether he is telling the truth or lying or playing a practical joke on his partner in the dialogue. If two people quarrel in a play, we, the audience, have to make up our minds as to who is in the right, who in the wrong in the matter. The author, the director, the actors may have furnished us with clues to aid our interpretation, but that, in the last resort, must remain our own. There is no reason why a spectator should not walk away from a performance of *Othello* convinced that Iago had been a much-wronged man in not having got preferment from Othello, and that Othello was a stupid brute to kill his wife on the slight suspicion thrown upon her. Indeed, there is no reason why a director should not produce the play in that way; but there might well be members of his audience who take away a different impression. Of course, skilful acting and direction, skilful writing, will be able to achieve a general consensus among the audience as to what the play is saying, yet each member of that audience will remain free to dissent and to stick to his own interpretation; if he does agree with the general impression that will be of his own free will.

Drama is also physically multi-dimensional: many things can happen at the same time (for example, what a character says may be contradicted by his gestures; two different groups of people may be doing different things at opposite ends of the stage, etc.). Narration on the printed page is necessarily linear, moving in a single dimension, so that at any given moment only one segment of the action can be concentrated upon, only a single thing can be happening. The technical mass media, where the director can steer the audience's attention through his use of the camera or microphone and through montage, are in this respect halfway between live theatre and the novel. But even in a single shot in a film the image can be far more multivalent than discursive narration: while the camera seemingly concentrates on one aspect, other important items of visual information may be present in the shot. One need only recall the final image of Orson Welles's *Citizen Kane* when the solution to the whole film's mystery is almost casually supplied by a glimpse of the word 'Rosebud' on the burning sleigh so that only spectators with a very keen eye and a real determination to see everything that is going on in each shot can go home with the correct solution to the film's puzzle.

Thus, in drama, the onus is on us, the audience, to find the meaning, arrive at our own interpretation of the action, the events we witness. That is why drama is more ambivalent than the novel, where, even when the author refrains from comment or interpretation, the linear sequence of events in the narration presents them in a sequence which already contains their significance. (There are, of course, novels like those of Ivy Compton-Burnett which are entirely in dialogue. But these are dramatic in essence—plays for reading).

This freedom of the audience in drama is the basis of another important phenomenon: the action on the stage is not merely multivalent and open to differing interpretations on its real, concrete level: it also acquires multivalence because its very concreteness makes interpretion possible on a number of different levels. A rose, as Gertrude Stein said, is a rose is a rose is a rose (i.e., a botanical specimen of a certain colour and scent and shape) but it can also be a symbol of love. If a rose is the

112

subject of a poem, its function as a symbol is usually clearly stated or at least very obviously implied by the poet; in a novel the function of the rose, if it is introduced into a narration, will also become fairly clear through its position in the line of narration. In drama that rose may be standing on the table in a vase and never be referred to: some members of the audience may see it just a prosaic part of the room's furniture, others may perceive it as a powerful image of love. And it may be neither or both. Similarly in the cinema an establishing shot of New York skyscrapers could be both a simple piece of expository information, telling us where the action of the film about to start will take place, yet at the same time it might be a powerful image of the heartlessness of that desert of stone, the titanic greed of the men who built such a city, etc. The fact is that such a shot does contain all that and infinitely more; like the real world itself it is open to infinite interpretation. If a playwright or film director wants it to be perceived as meaning a specific thing, he will need all his skill to make that clear. Yet it will continue to mean a great many different things as well.

This is the source of one of the most intriguing and mysterious aspects of drama—that dramatic works can contain meanings of which their authors must almost certainly have been unaware. Take early silent slapstick film comedies. Almost certainly these were devised by their creators (Chaplin, Keaton, Harry Langdon, Harold Lloyd) simply as sequences of visual gags with only one purpose in mind, to make audiences laugh. Today they can—quite correctly—be seen and interpreted as images of the helpless individual in industrial society being kicked around by the authorities and, indeed, tyrannised by the mechanical devices of his own creation. The quite naively invented gags have thus acquired the status of profound social comment. By looking for and finding mishaps which can arise from being in contact with motor cars, conveyor belts, mechanical ladders and other tools of this kind, the creators of these comedies had assembled a veritable museum of the pitfalls of mechanical gadgetry. Each of these possible mishaps contained a truth about the particular gadget's potential of mischief. And because the truth is multi-dimensional, that truth automatically contained all other truths connected with its subject-matter, including the more general comment on society.

Conversely, on a much higher plane: Hamlet's relationship with his mother can today be commented upon as a profound and truthful representation of the Oedipus complex, a matter Shakespeare could not possibly have been aware of. Faced with having to depict—because his source demanded it—the relationship between a young man and his mother whom he suspects of adultery, the playwright had to imagine the feelings such a situation would provoke. In doing so he had to draw on his own feelings, or what he imagined his own feelings might have been had he himself been in a similar situation. Having succeeded in doing this with the utmost truthfulness and possessing the skill to set it down in the clearest and subtlest language, Shakespeare preserved an emotion of great complexity and truthfulness, and that emotion can then be analysed through concepts of which he was totally unaware. To a future epoch with even more profound scientific insights into human nature, the same dramatic text embodying that complex emotion may yield other insights of which we have no inkling. Drama at its best, in the concreteness, the reality, of its nature, has the infinite complexity of the real world itself.

Action on the level of reality (the comic struggling

with a recalcitrant motor car) can therefore at the same time be a poetic metaphor (man enmeshed in the tentacles of the machine). There is a third level as well: that of the author's fantasy life (the author's feelings of inadequacy when faced with his car; his nightmare of being a motorist).

The tensions between these three levels and their subtle interaction in the spectator's conscious as well as subconscious mind have been used by dramatists of all epochs. In ancient Greek tragedy the choral passages pointed to the general truths of which the particular situations of the plot were the embodiments. Medieval allegorical drama presented many of its characters as personifications of general principles, but the audiences enjoyed their antics as the actions of highly individualised characters: the Vice of Lechery would also be recognised as a particular lecher well known in that community; the poetic metaphor would, at the same time, be a very concrete realistic case.

A play like Shakespeare's *Winter's Tale* works on all three levels: it tells a story to be followed naively as a good yarn of passion and adventure; it is an allegory, a moral parable about jealousy, selfishness and forgiveness; and it is also a 'wish-fulfilment fantasy' of its author, a dream image of the return of lost love and the redemption of past guilt.

In our own more self-conscious age, playwrights are making more deliberate use of the existence and interaction of these three (or at least three) levels. A work like Harold Pinter's *The Homecoming* is at one and the same time brutally realistic, a picture of a family of pimps and prostitutes, a wish-fulfilment dream of the son's sexual conquest of the mother, and a poetic metaphor of man lost in the inhumanity of a society founded on greed. The

115

same playwright's *Old Times* presents a situation which could be real (the visit of a long-absent woman friend of the wife) but which might be merely the husband's nightmare about what might happen if such a long-absent friend did come to visit his wife; it might (there are hints in the way the play is written but no definite clue is given) be merely a kind of game played by three people who indulge in this pastime of private fantasy; and it is, of course, inevitably, an expression of the author's own nightmare of ageing, jealousy and the fallibility of memory. It is or might be all this, or more; all we have is a sequence of events and dialogues which unfold in front of our eyes: we are free to make of it what we want.

The work of writers like Beckett, Arrabal or Edward Bond is open to similarly multivalent interpretation. The playwrights in this type of drama firmly believe in the realism, the truth, of fantasy.

There has in the last decades been a great deal of controversy among modern playwrights and critics about realism, truth and political commitment in drama. In France particularly, left-wing playwrights and critics, gathered under the banner of Brecht, have attacked the so-called Absurdists (Beckett, Ionesco) for their neglect of social issues, while Ionesco has retaliated by calling the Brechtians propagandists who distorted the truth in the interest of their political cause.

In the light of the considerations I have tried to offer here I think this is a false controversy: the politically and socially oriented playwrights are simply concentrating their intentions on external reality (political conditions, social problems, etc.) while the introspectively poetic playwrights such as Beckett or Ionesco tend to neglect the 'realities' of social circumstances and their documentation in favour of an inner truth. Their plays are dreams rather than photographs of the external world. But these dreams are as real to them—and to audiences—as the external realities are to the Brechtians. And indeed they have political implications as potent as the social realism of those interested in the external world. *Waiting for Godot*, which is about disappointed expectations, has had its political impact in places as far apart as Algeria and Poland. Landless Algerian peasants saw Godot who never comes as the often promised but never delivered land reform; and audiences in Poland with its history of subjection to other nations, responded with the unanimous opinion that Godot was the national freedom and independence so often denied them. That *Waiting for Godot* had this impact is due to the reality and truth of the inner—as against the outward—action and theme of the play: ultimately it dramatises a state of mind, the psychological reality, the 'feel' of the emotion of unfulfilled expectancy when one is waiting for something which has been promised but fails to materialise.

As a means of expression and communication, drama—quite apart from telling stories or providing models of social situations in action—is to a very considerable extent concerned with the recreation of human states of emotion, with letting audiences partake in emotions that would otherwise be denied them, and is a means of widening their experience as human beings and extending their capacity to feel richer, subtler, more elevated emotions. The truth of drama thus appears on a multiplicity of levels. The play which communicates to us important lessons about social behaviour, which tells us a gripping story, may also open up unknown areas of emotional experience through powerful poetic images. The plays of so socially conscious a playwright as Brecht, who was dedicated to the task of showing his fellow human beings that the world must be changed through social action, also contain powerful poetic metaphors of human emotion. Mother Courage pulling her cart, Grusche in *The Caucasian Chalk Circle* crossing the swaying bridge over the ravine to save the child, Galileo indulging himself with goose-liver—these are poetic images of human resilience, tenderness and sensuality as truly as the barren tree with its waiting figures in *Waiting for Godot* is an image of the emptiness of human existence.

Drama is as multifaceted in its images, as ambivalent in its meanings, as the world it mirrors. That is its main strength, its characteristic as a mode of expression—and its greatness.

Index of plays

General index

Abbey Theatre, Dublin 30
Absurdist theatre 65, 117
action 9, 14, 17, 18, 24, 27, 29,
  35, 40-41, 43, 46-7, 51-3,
  72, 74, 79, 80, 82, 88, 109,
  111, 113-16, 118
actors (performers) 11, 16,
  23-5, 33-6, 41, 46-9, 51-2,
  55-6, 60, 64, 70, 72, 79, 84,
  88-92, 94, 102, 112, 118
Adamov, Arthur, 58-9
Altman, Robert 48
Antonioni, Michelangelo 48
Arrabal, Fernando 117
Arts Council of Great Britain
  96
audience(s) 15, 18, 23-7, 29,
  31-3, 35-9, 41, 44-5, 48-9,
  53, 55, 64, 69, 71-3, 75-6,
  79, 80-85, 88-9, 92-4, 97-8,
  100-103, 110, 112-14, 116,
  118
author(s) 14, 17, 23, 34-7, 39,
  44, 73, 92-3, 97-8, 107-8,
  111-17
avant-garde theatre 93, 102-3

ballet 11, 28, 43, 86, 90
Beaumarchais, Pierre A. 32
Beck, Julian 94
Beckett, Samuel 19, 22, 36, 44,
  48, 58, 75-6, 82, 84, 93, 117
behaviour, behaviour pat-
  terns 19, 20-22, 66, 74, 104,
  118
Benjamin, Walter, 12
Bergman, Ingmar 78
Bergson, Henri 71
Bolt, Robert 78, 84
Bond, Edward 117
Brecht, Bertolt 22, 35, 63-6,
  75-7, 79, 84, 92-3, 100, 117,
  119
Brentano, Clemens 58
Brook, Peter 89
Buchner, Georg 74
burlesque 67
Burton, Richard 89

Camus, Albert 22
Carné, Marcel 33
Chaplin, Charles 33, 71, 75,
  114

121

General index